"David Dockery continues to define the essential features of Christ-centered education in ways that make us want to stand up and cheer. At a time when pragmatism seems to rule, Dockery exhorts us to keep moving ahead with our eyes on the horizon. This work will certainly become the standard for explaining the vision for all of us in Christ-centered education."

Bill Brown
President, Cedarville University

"There's no greater need for the church than to equip the coming generation of Christians to engage the postmodern culture. My friend David Dockery has given us an excellent resource for that effort. His new book challenges the academy to make biblical worldview the foundation for not only renewing minds but developing character. This is a timely and valuable resource."

Charles W. Colson
Founder, Prison Fellowship

"David Dockery is one of my heroes, quietly going about producing a prolific body of writing, with fresh insight and deep conviction, all the while leading one of our finest Christian universities. This book speaks out of a deep reservoir of long and faithful experience in the Christian academy. He captures it all, collecting in this one place the historic and noble commitments of Christian higher education, providing for us thoughtful foundations on which to envision the future. What I like most about this book is the unreserved passion about the possibilities ahead for the Christian university. I share that passion, and I am grateful to David Dockery for his strong voice in our midst."

Philip W. Eaton, President
Seattle Pacific University

D1550414

"*Renewing Minds* is a robust and thoughtful defense of the necessity and ideals of Christian higher education, coupled with a shrewd and wise assessment of the challenges and strategies of the future."

Alister E. McGrath
Professor of Historical Theology
Oxford University

"David Dockery is a rare combination of serious scholar, experienced academic leader, and Christian intellectual. In *Renewing Minds* he combines these roles and sets out a bold agenda for Christian higher education. This is an important and timely book that will challenge Christians to recover an authentically Christian vision of education, intellect, and learning."

R. Albert Mohler Jr., President
The Southern Baptist Theological Seminary

"David Dockery writes with passion and hope as one of the world's leading thinkers and visionaries in Christian higher education.

"Were it in my power I would put a copy of this book in the hands of every professor and administrator in Christian higher education.

"As it is, every chair, dean, and new faculty member at Baylor University will receive this treasure, which boldly calls us to faithfulness to our Christ-centered mission."

J. Randall O'Brien
Executive Vice President and Provost
Baylor University

"Visionary and magisterial, Dockery's big-picture manifesto vividly blocks in the demanding standards, proper cultural contextualizing, and strategic global significance of thoroughgoing Christian higher education today. The Bible-anchored argumentation convinces the head, and the writer's zeal warms the heart. This is in every way a landmark book!"

J. I. Packer
Professor of Theology, Regent College

"David Dockery once again demonstrates why he is one of the leading visionaries in Christian higher education. I can foresee *Renewing Minds* as the standard for faculty and administrators in Christian colleges and universities in the years ahead. This volume could not be more timely as it assesses the current state well but, with visionary acumen, looks to the future with keen strategic thinking."

Thom S. Rainer
President and CEO
LifeWay Christian Resources

"David Dockery has accomplished the truly remarkable: providing a comprehensive systematic foundation for expressing biblical principles in higher education in a style and format that is both intellectually respectable yet fully accessible. This volume could well become required reading for a generation of administrators and faculty at Christian colleges and universities. The extensive bibliography on integrating faith and scholarship is itself worth the price of the book."

Carl Zylstra
President, Dordt College

RENEWING MINDS

RENEWING MINDS

Serving Church and Society through
Christian Higher Education

DAVID S. DOCKERY

Foreword by Robert P. George, Princeton University

ACADEMIC

NASHVILLE, TENNESSEE

978–0–8054–4495–7

Published by B&H Publishing Group
Nashville, Tennessee

Dewey Decimal Classification: 378
Subject Heading: CHRISTIAN EDUCATION \
HIGHER EDUCATION

1 2 3 4 5 6 7 8 9 10 11 12 • 16 15 14 13 12 11 10 09 08 07
VP

To

Jon and Sarah
Ben and Julie
Tim and Andrea

"Be transformed by the
renewing of your mind, so that
you may discern what is the
good, pleasing, and perfect will of God"
Romans 12:2

Contents

Foreword

Christian colleges and universities operate today in a broader intellectual milieu in which secularist forms of rationalism are ascendant. The "cultured despisers" of religion regard faith, Christian faith in particular, as irrational and obscurantist. They consider that it may be necessary to tolerate and perhaps even accommodate faith on campus by providing or recognizing denominational chaplaincies, student religious groups, and so forth. But religious faith, even when tolerated, is understood as at best irrelevant to, and at worst incompatible with, serious and unfettered intellectual inquiry and the transmission of knowledge to students.

Even where a more enlightened attitude toward faith prevails, rarely is religion conceived as something that serves, or can serve, the cause of learning. Perhaps religion is understood as providing consolation and emotional support for students and even occasionally for faculty members who need that sort of thing or go in for it. In circumstances particularly friendly to religion, faith might be viewed as providing a kind of inspiration and perhaps even certain types of moral guidance. Occasionally one even finds religion treated as supplying something pertaining to a distinct spiritual element of the human person that requires pastoral tending in a way roughly parallel to the way in which physical fitness is tended to on campuses by offering athletic opportunities of various sorts under the supervision of coaches and trainers. Religion, in short, is at most an extracurricular activity—one among many offered on campus.

How, then, in the concrete circumstances of contemporary intellectual life, should avowedly Christian institutions of higher learning understand themselves and their mission? What is the way forward for Christ-centered colleges and universities?

There are three leading options.

The first might be called the way of *assimilation.* Institutions choosing this option will seek, in substance, to emulate the most successful and prestigious secular colleges and universities, many of which themselves began as Christian institutions but gradually abandoned their religious identity. Of course, one expects that Christian institutions choosing this option will want to retain more of their religious heritage than has been retained by, say, Harvard or Yale (or my own institution, Princeton), but they will seek to do it by trying to maintain a more faith-friendly campus environment and by offering richer extracurricular religious activities. Catholic institutions may feature Sunday and even daily mass in the college chapel and keep the custom of placing crucifixes in classrooms. Protestant colleges might encourage Bible clubs, mission trips during spring break, and the like. The key thing is that religion at these institutions, like religion at secular institutions, will be seen as essentially extracurricular rather than as something integrally connected with the mission of acquiring and transmitting knowledge.

The second option might be called the way of *isolation.* Colleges and universities that opt for this path will seek, in effect, to withdraw from the broader intellectual culture, viewing it as irredeemably corrupt and implacably hostile to Christian faith. Fearing that exposure to secular rationalist currents will erode faith on campus and lure faculty and students away from Christ, leaders of institutions who opt for isolation will view themselves as preserving the intellectual and spiritual treasures that are our Christian patrimony by removing them to the equivalent of monasteries in the new Dark Ages. Religion will remain integral to the scholarly enterprise and to the college curriculum, but one can only expect that the thrust of intellectual activity will be toward preserving, and not towards critically and creatively building upon, what has been bequeathed to us by the great Christian scholars who have gone before and the traditions of thought and inquiry they founded and nurtured. Moreover, scholarship generated in such institutions will not critically engage the broader intellectual culture, nor will students taught in them be well equipped to do battle in that culture.

The third possibility is the one proposed by the distinguished author of the book you are blessed to have in your hands, David S. Dockery. This option might be called the way of *engagement.* It is not only preached by David Dockery; he is one of its most dynamic and successful practitioners. Under his leadership, Union University has elected neither the way of assimilation to the secular rationalism of the broader intellectual culture nor isolation from it. Rather, Union has chosen to engage the broader culture from the perspective of Christian faith, understood not as a mere means of consolation and emotional support but as an integral part of the intellectual enterprise. Dockery does share with those who would opt for isolationism one thing: the conviction that faith is no mere extracurricular activity. The richness of the Christian intellectual tradition—rooted in the Bible and expounded and developed by the great thinkers of the patristic period, the high middle ages, the Renaissance and Reformation, and en the modern period—is living proof of the power of faith to illumine the intellectual landscape and play a key role in the central mission of the university: inquiry in pursuit of truth.

Engagement requires confidence, confidence in the truths of Christian faith and confidence in the ability of Christian scholars and students to grow richer in knowledge and in faith by critically engaging an intellectual culture that is less than hospitable to the Christian worldview. It is confidence of precisely this sort that enables Dockery to declare that "we need more than new ideas and enhanced programs; we need the kind of tough-minded thinking that results in culture-engaging living." Where this confidence is absent, cultural engagement is simply not possible. Where it is present, Christians can fruitfully enter into discussion and debate with secular (and even secularist) intellectuals across the range of scholarly disciplines, demanding nothing but intellectual honesty and openness to argument. Where there is mutual goodwill, even people who disagree about fundamental matters can learn from one another. Christians, for example, can have their knowledge and faith enriched—not eroded—by thinking carefully about challenges to faith presented by secularist colleagues who, despite their unbelief, share with Christian intellectuals a desire to know the truth and to gain a richer understanding of the way things in fact are. So Christians who share Dockery's belief in the virtues of engagement will understand that they have something to teach but also something to learn in the process of engaging those who accept what I have labeled the "secularist orthodoxy."

Those who join David Dockery on the path of engagement, whether their Christian confession is Catholic or Protestant, will affirm with the late Pope John Paul II the integration of faith and reason in the quest for knowledge. "Faith and reason are," the Pope said, "two wings upon which the human spirit ascends to contemplation of the truth." Faith, far from being the enemy of reason, is its indispensable ally. But the obverse is also true. Just as reason needs faith, faith requires reason. In the life of faith itself, reason is by no means superfluous. As David Dockery reminds us, our Lord Himself strictly enjoined us to love God not only with our hearts and souls but also with our minds. That is why it is the calling of the Christian college and university to be constantly and resolutely about the business of *renewing minds*.

Robert P. George
McCormick Professor of Jurisprudence
Princeton University

Preface

~~~~~~

R enewing Minds: Serving Church and Society through Christian Higher Education is an introduction to the field of Christian higher education. Drawing on the words of the apostle Paul in Romans 12:2, the book, as the title suggests, focuses on the distinctive role of Christian higher education, both in the kingdom of God and in the world of the academy. It is written for administrators, trustees, church leaders, faculty, and staff who are beginning their service with or relationship to a Christ-centered institution. It is also written for students or parents of students who are considering a Christian college or university. It is not a lengthy book, but it does provide pointers to additional sources for those who wish to read more about these important matters.

For almost twenty-five years I have been involved in Christian higher education as a faculty member or administrator. During some of those years, I was focused in the realm of theological education. For nearly a dozen of those years, I have served as president of Union University (founded in 1823), a Christian university with a long history in the liberal arts tradition. I have great appreciation for seminaries, Bible colleges, and even colleges and universities with some ongoing or historic church relationship. But this book, while having application to various kinds of institutions, is an explication of the identity and mission of Christian colleges and universities that desire to be intentional about their purpose. My own thinking about what this "intentional" focus means has developed over the years. This book represents those reflections.

The number of people who have influenced my thinking are many. While I hesitate to mention any of them because others will be left out, I must acknowledge the trustees, faculty, staff, students and administrators at Union University who have been God's gift to me since December 8, 1995. Others who have been significant in the development of my thinking and whose ideas can be found at various places throughout this book include the late Carl Henry and Ted Engstrom. Also, I must acknowledge the important impact of Jay Kesler, Bob Agee, Bob Andringa, James Sire, Chuck Colson, Paul Corts, and many more. I thank God for each one of them and for their influence on my life.

The writings of George Marsden, James Burtchaell, Arthur Holmes, Mark Schwenn, Mark Roche, Duane Litfin, and Timothy George among others, have greatly shaped my understanding of the important and distinctive mission of Christian higher education. While all of these have influenced this work, probably even in ways that I am not aware, I must take responsibility for the shortcomings found in the book.

Portions of almost every chapter have been previously presented at Union University and in other settings as well. The feedback offered from those in attendance on those occasions has been most helpful. On the acknowledgments page I have noted these places. I want to thank those responsible for the gracious invitations to make presentations on these campuses and in other contexts. I am honored that they have given me these privileges, and I thank them for their part in developing this work.

Several people have contributed to the various stages of the preparation of this manuscript. My deep gratitude is offered to Greg Thornbury, Hal Poe, Jimmy Davis, Gene Fant, Carla Sanderson, Todd Brady, Barbara McMillin, Charles Fowler, Rich Grimm, Beverly Burrow, Tim Ellsworth,

Tom Rosebrough, Cindy Meredith, and Melanie Rickman. I am thankful for the valuable input that they have provided, but particularly do I want to thank Melanie Rickman, Cindy Meredith, and Greg Thornbury. The book has been greatly strengthened by their able contributions. I want to thank John Landers and Ray Clendenen for their editorial efforts and for the support that they, along with Thom Rainer, have offered for this project. The encouragement from the Union University board of trustees has meant more than I can express. The willingness of Robby George to write the Foreword for this book is an incredible gift. Dr. George, who holds the prestigious McCormick Chair of Jurisprudence at Princeton University, is one of the truly outstanding thinkers in today's Academy. His contribution to this book, like his friendship, is priceless.

Finally, I want to offer my deepest expression of gratitude to my family. Lanese has endured yet one more writing project. Without her love and kind encouragement, this project would not have been possible. I am also grateful for the support provided by Jon and Sarah, Ben and Julie, and Tim and Andrea, to whom this book is affectionately dedicated.

I offer this book with the prayer and hope that it might be used to advance the work of Christian higher education and to strengthen the work of campuses in this country and around the world. If that happens in any measure, I will be grateful to our great and glorious God.

Soli Deo Gloria

David S. Dockery is president of Union University in Jackson, Tennessee. He has served as chairman of the board of the Council for Christian Colleges and Universities. He also has served on the board of the Consortium for Global Education, Christianity Today, and the Tennessee Independent Colleges and Universities Association. Dockery is the author or editor of more than twenty-five books including *Biblical Interpretation Then and Now*, *Theologians of the Baptist Tradition*, the *Holman Bible Handbook*, and *Shaping a Christian Worldview*. He also serves as a contributing editor for Christianity Today and as the associate general editor of the *New American Commentary*.

Acknowledgments

- Portions of chapters 1–8 were previously given as addresses at Union University and were included in the Union University projects titled *The Future of Christian Higher Education* and *Shaping a Christian Worldview*.
- Portions of chapter 1 were previously published by the Ethics and Religious Liberty Commission; in the *Southern Baptist Journal of Theology* 1 (1997); in *Faith and Mission* 18 (2000); and by the Wilberforce Forum of Prison Fellowship.
- Portions of chapter 2 were presented as the keynote address at the presidential inauguration of Evans Whitaker, Anderson University.
- Portions of chapter 3 were presented at Houston Baptist University, the University of Mobile, the Alabama Baptist Leadership Conference, and the annual meeting of the Association of Southern Baptist Colleges and Schools.
- Portions of chapter 4 were prepared for lectures at Biola University, at Louisiana College, and at the annual meeting of the Southern Association of Colleges and Schools.
- Portions of chapters 3 and 5 were presented at Azusa Pacific University, Oklahoma Baptist University, and Oklahoma Christian University.

- Portions of chapters 6 and 7 were presented at the annual Faculty Development Conference of the Council for Christian Colleges and Universities.
- Portions of chapter 8 were presented at Baylor University, Midwestern Baptist Theological Seminary, the annual meeting of the Association of Southern Baptist Colleges and Schools, and published as a chapter in *The Future of Baptist Higher Education*.
- A portion of chapter 9 was presented at the annual meeting of the Consortium for Global Education.
- Several others have influenced portions of each chapter, and their work is listed in the sources at the conclusion of each of the chapters.

1

Loving God with Our Minds

"Love the Lord your God with all your heart,
with all your soul, and with all your mind."

~Matthew 22:37

"In Augustine's view the incentive for so much learning is
not then by any means mere mastery of knowledge for its
own sake; such ambition 'puffs up' the mind and makes it
an object of idolatrous worship. What prompts earnest and
excellent scholarship in the Christian is the 'fear of the Lord.'"

David Lyle Jeffrey, The People of the Book

"We cannot neglect the soulful development
of a Christian mind."

J. P. Moreland, Love God
with All Your Mind

"Christ wants a child's heart, but a grown-up's head."

C. S. Lewis, Mere Christianity

The world as we know and experience it in many ways began again on September 12, 2001. We now live with a global awareness and new understandings of terrorism, war, and the meaning of security. As we look around the globe, we observe a shift among the nations that will influence this new century. Futurists are suggesting that China and India are the countries to watch for future economic influence, while places like Nigeria, Brazil, and South Korea will be the sources of strength for a "new Christendom" whose numerical predominance will be located in the Southern hemisphere. These changes require those involved in the work of Christian higher education to look at the future differently than we did just a decade ago.

Current Challenges

Moreover, the changes in higher education seem to be ever-shifting in terms of philosophy, methodology, and delivery system possibilities. It is impossible to keep up with these changes, but we must continue to monitor these trends and provide education that is faithful to our heritage as Christ-centered institutions while seeking to be ever more connected to the reformulations of the world in which we now find ourselves. These changes are manifold and can be summarized in terms of technology; education delivery systems; the rise of for-profit institutions along the landscape of higher education; and the interface between traditional education and the rest of society in terms of internships, classroom consulting, service learning, distance learning, and strategic institutional alliances. All of these cause us to rethink traditional classroom boundaries.

Special interest groups can be expected to offer pressure for higher education institutions to conform on issues that will compromise our mission. We must anticipate that issues of sexuality, sexual freedom, and same-gender unions could impact federal funding and possible accreditation matters for some private church-related institutions. The right to hire will likely be the most important legal issue that Christian colleges and universities face in the near future. These and other issues make the challenges of providing Christ-centered higher education in the twenty-first century more challenging than ever before.

With these factors in mind, we must think wisely, carefully, strategically, and creatively as we look toward the future to enable Christian colleges and universities to become more thoroughly mission driven, grounded in our commitment to offer education that is academically rigorous and unapologetically Christian as we seek to become resources for serious Christian thinking and scholarship in all disciplines for the initial decades of the twenty-first century.

We do so while taking into account the shifts and challenges in our society, in culture at large, in denominational landscapes, in our nation, and in our world. Yet we must not be naïve or deceived. Our world is still plagued by the effects of the fall. The New Testament reminds us that sin has not just impacted individuals; it has impacted creation as well. Since the time when humanity was banished from the garden, disarray and disorder have characterized the earth. The book of Romans claims that creation has been subjected to futility through humanity's sin, though there is hope in the work of Christ.

Until the ultimate redemption of the earth is accomplished, we live with the essential disorder of human life that remains all around us. Newspapers tell us each day that new diseases are discovered, and they afflict thousands around the world. New forms of injustice are contrived and carried out upon the unsuspecting each day. New configurations of suffering are documented daily. Yet we have hope not because of our combined abilities, intelligence, or cleverness but because Jesus Christ has come to this world and by His life, death, resurrection, and exaltation we have and should focus on a hopeful future.

We cannot forget the pull of the world or the pull to ignore God so evident all around us. As Christ-followers we are not called out of this fallen world, but we are called to engage it and to sanctify the ongoing secular society in which we live. I believe this is the reality of incarnational Christianity. It is the pattern of truth found in Christ Himself. That being the case, there is no sphere of humanity to which Jesus Christ is irrelevant; and certainly that includes the academic world, which is the focus of this book. The incarnation and resurrection of Jesus Christ provide the foundations of a Christian worldview that have cosmic consequences for the way we understand our world and engage the culture in which we live.

A Different Approach to Higher Education

In light of these challenges, I want to propose a different approach to thinking about truth and higher education. I believe that the integration of faith and learning is the essence of authentic Christian higher education and should be wholeheartedly implemented across the campus and across the curriculum. This was once the goal of almost every college in America. This is no longer the case. Before the nineteenth century every college started in this country, with the exception of the University of Pennsylvania and the University of Virginia, was a Christian-based institution committed to revealed truth. All of that changed with the rise of secularization and specialization, creating dualisms of every kind—a separation of head knowledge from heart knowledge, faith from learning, revealed truth from observed truth, and careers from vocation.

What happened was a loss of an integrated worldview in the academy. There was a failure to see that every discipline and every specialization could be and should be approached from the vantage point of faith, the foundational building block for a Christian worldview. The separation of faith from learning and teaching was the first step toward creating a confused and disconnected approach to higher education, even in church-related institutions.

Historical Overview

A brief overview of Christian higher education will help us see the shifts and changes in purpose and focus across the years. Early Christian education emphasized catechetical purposes as foundational. Medieval universities (those developed between the eleventh and fifteenth centuries) were largely for the purposes of professional education, with some general education for the elite. Of the seventy-nine universities in existence in Europe during this time, Salerno was best known for medicine, Bologna for law, and Paris for theology.

The Renaissance envisioned the revival of Greek and Roman literature while newer subjects were developing during the medieval periods such as arithmetic, geometry, and music. The Reformation and post-Reformation period placed all aspects of education within the context of a Christian worldview. American higher education reached its zenith, building on what had gone before. Early American colleges governed by trustees from related religious groups provided education within the context of faith and grounded in the pursuit of truth (*veritas*). Some of these schools included:

Institution/ Location	Date Founded	Denomination
Harvard (Massachusetts)	1636	Congregational
William and Mary (Virginia)	1693	Anglican
Yale (Connecticut)	1701	Congregational
Princeton (New Jersey)	1746	New Light Presbyterian
Columbia (New York)	1754	Anglican
Brown (Rhode Island)	1764	Baptist
Rutgers (New Jersey)	1765	Dutch Reformed

Pennsylvania and Virginia were essentially the first secular institutions. The German model espousing research and academic freedom began to influence American higher education in the nineteenth century. Johns Hopkins, founded in Maryland in 1867, was the first purely research institution in this country.

During the nineteenth century, state-supported higher education began to flourish, following the University of Virginia model, which had separated theological influence from the curriculum by abolishing the chair of divinity in its initial reorganization. The University of Michigan adopted a credit point system; Harvard introduced an elective curriculum; and majors and specializations followed as we moved into the twentieth century.

The rise of Enlightenment thought was a watershed in the history of Western civilization; it was a time when the Christian consensus was broken by a radical secular spirit. The Enlightenment philosophy stressed the primacy of nature, a high view of reason and a low view of sin, and an antisupernatural bias; and it encouraged revolt against a faith-affirming perspective on education. Friedrich Schleiermacher's *On Religion: Speeches to Its Cultural Despisers* severed faith from philosophy and morality. Faith was understood only in pietistic terms, having little connection with matters of truth. Though Schleiermacher tried to save the Christian faith, in reality faith was separated from the exploration of truth—even the Jesus of history and the study of the Bible was separated from the "Christ of faith."

Early twentieth-century American education was impacted by this mind-set in the modernist-fundamentalist controversies. Both groups in various ways tried to save "faith" through various pietistic approaches; on the one hand you could find the separatistic pietism of American fundamentalism, and on the other there was the pragmatic pietism of William James, the common-faith civil religion of John Dewey, and the historical-experiential religion of Harry Emerson Fosdick. The result, however, was the divorce of faith from teaching and scholarship in universities across the country in the arts, the humanities, the sciences, the social sciences, and all other spheres, including the scholarly study of religion.

During this time there remained a belief in a transcultural objective truth in all fields, but the dominant perspective, with rare exceptions, maintained that faith had to be bracketed from this search for truth. The situation changed even more drastically at the end of the twentieth century with the rise of postmodernism, which includes the loss of a belief in normative truth and the influence of relativism in almost all spheres of knowledge.

Following World War II, a rapid expansion of higher education took place all across America. As we enter the twenty-first century, there are approximately 2,500 four-year institutions of higher learning. In addition there are about 1,000 community colleges and several hundred for-profit institutions. Many public institutions are large research universities. Of the 1,600 private institutions, almost 800 maintain some church relationship (about 400 mainline Protestant; a little less than 300 Roman Catholic; and slightly more than 100 Evangelical). Among these 800 schools, we can identify four different types:

The Private College

- independent in its operation,
- few Christian commitments,
- faculty and students (with some or many trustees) probably unrelated to the Christian heritage of the college, and
- approach to education generally as diverse and pluralistic as most public institutions.

The Bible College

- preparation for church-related vocations,
- generally study only Christian material, and
- undergraduate seminary.

The Church-Related College

- acknowledgment of Christian heritage,
- sees itself as an academic partner with its sponsoring denomination, with many faculty, students, and board members coming from that tradition,
- approach to education is characterized by two generally unrelated spheres (often called the "two-sphere approach"): (a) campus ministry and chapel programs, and (b) academic curriculum and program and caring context for education.

The Systemic or Intentional Christian College or University in the Liberal Arts Tradition

- strong cultural ties with sponsoring denomination/ constituency,
- faculty and students conscious of denominational/ constituency ties,
- trustee board has strong tie to denomination/ constituency,
- provides opportunity for examination of subject matter from a faith perspective,
- grace-filled context for education,
- approach to education grounded in Christian world-view and life view, and
- education as a learning community—one sphere characterized by the integration of faith and learning and faith and living.

Now we find ourselves at the beginning of the twenty-first century. What approach to education can we or should we expect from colleges and universities that maintain their Christian identity? In the relativistic world in which we find ourselves, can we expect or should we expect an explicit Christian mission to be maintained? Can the "one-sphere" systemic approach to the integration of faith and learning be articulated and practiced, or is the "two-sphere" dualistic church-related model a better strategy? We believe that the integration of faith and learning is at the essence of authentic Christian higher education and should be wholeheartedly implemented across the campus and across the curriculum.

In thinking about Christian higher education, we cannot rapidly leap over the foundational issues. We need to think carefully and intentionally about the importance of inte-

University, proposes several reforms meant to alter the culture of American academic life. He recognizes the changes that have been brought about in higher education through the rise and expansion of the specialized disciplines. Yet he proposes that the problem we face is not necessarily increasing academic specialization but the lack of interrelatedness between the disciplines. This unwillingness to relate disciplines to one another has resulted in a fragmentation of knowledge. The fragmentation of knowledge should alarm all who are committed to Christian higher education, for it strikes at the foundation of our purpose.

Damrosch calls for an interdisciplinary community approach to teaching and research, simultaneously generalizing *and* specializing. He discourages the isolationism of the academy, urges the university to reshape itself by working in concert across established field boundaries. He rightly recognizes that disciplinary fragmentation dates from decisions made only a century ago when the modern American university assumed its current form.

Damrosch's suggestions are noble and helpful but short-sighted. They fail to address the most important aspect of the problem, which is not specialization per se but a specialization brought on by a fragmentation of knowledge. This fragmentation has resulted in a false dichotomy between the life of the mind and the life of faith. Christian institutions seeking to put into practice the implications of the Great Commandment can enter this important conversation.

I would suggest that the starting point of loving God with our minds, thinking Christianly, points us to a unity of knowledge, a seamless whole, because all true knowledge flows from the one Creator to His one creation. Thus specific bodies of knowledge relate to one another not just because scholars work together in community, not just because interdisciplinary work broadens our knowledge, but because all truth has its source in God, composing a single universe of knowledge.

Then education will mean much more than passing on content to our students. It will also mean shaping character, and it will move toward the development and construction of a convictional worldview by which we can see, learn, and interpret the world from the vantage point of God's revelation to us. We must therefore seek to build Christian liberal arts universities where men and women can be introduced to an understanding and appreciation of God, His creation and grace, and humanity's place of privilege and responsibility in God's world.

Understanding and Appreciating Our Heritage

It is helpful to realize that the goal of Christian education, rightly understood for the past two thousand years, has been this faith and knowledge integration. The starting point for this integration has rested not only on the foundation of the words of Jesus' Great Commandment but also on the wisdom literature of the Hebrew Scriptures, which reminds us that the fear of the Lord is the beginning of knowledge, wisdom, and understanding (Prov 1:7; Ps 111:10; Job 28:28). Thus the beginning point for thinking, learning, and teaching is our reverence before God the Father Almighty, Maker of heaven and earth.

The search for knowledge, the quest for truth—phrases so familiar as to be clichés in education—must not be uttered carelessly. For when we speak of such from the Christian perspective, we speak of God who is omniscience, God who is truth. From this foundation has followed a legacy of those committed to a passion for learning based on the supposition

that all truth is God's truth. Thus, as Christians related together in a learning community, we all as faculty, students,
staff, and administrators are to seek to take every thought captive to Christ and love God with all our minds.

Perhaps Justin Martyr, a philosopher in the second century (AD 100–165), was the first in postapostolic times to
articulate the need for faith *and* learning. He said that whatever has been uttered aright by any person in any place belongs to us Christians. In Alexandria in the next century,
both Clement and Origen instructed their converts not only
in doctrine but in science, literature, and philosophy as well.
Finally, Augustine penned the thought that every true and
good Christian should understand that wherever we may find
truth, it is the Lord's.

This legacy may be observed across the centuries and in
most every culture, for wherever the gospel has been received,
the academy and Christian learning have followed. For example, when commenting on the place of the humanities, John
Calvin reflected: "If we regard the Spirit of God as the sole
fountain of truth, we shall neither reject the truth itself, nor
despise it wherever it shall appear, unless we wish to dishonor
the Spirit of God. For by holding the gifts of the Spirit in
slight esteem, we condemn and reproach the Spirit Himself"
(*Institutes* 2.2.15).

Calvin's contemporaries Luther and Erasmus, though with
different emphases, underscored Calvin's convictions. Erasmus
maintained: "All studies, philosophy, rhetoric, [and literature]
are followed for this one object, that we know Christ and hon-
or Him. This is the end of all learning and eloquence" (cited
by Lockerbie, *Thinking and Acting like a Christian*, 92–93).

The commitment of Erasmus and Calvin to a program of
studies so single-mindedly Christ-centered provides a model

for us as we seek to bring faith to bear upon all learning and living. Their sense of wholeness in studies and teaching, in art and science, in ethics and etiquette, in politics and government, provides a striking model for us.

We must seek to become heirs of this great legacy, moving toward becoming Great Commandment colleges and universities by seeking to understand and cherish God's revelation and holy creation in our discipline-related explorations.

The Great Commandment: Applications

Being Great Commandment institutions means more than the integration of faith and learning; it involves the integration of faith and living. Jesus tells us to apply our love for God with heart, mind, and soul by loving others. Divine love issues in interpersonal love. Such application extends to work and school, home and church, politics and play. It impacts the most elemental aspects of our daily lives—for all thinking must be accompanied by action—thinking and acting Christianly.

This means we will seek to serve one another by demonstrating the love of God to students, colleagues, and others. We will show love and respect for those we serve. We will attempt to work for their highest good. Following the observations of Francis Schaeffer, we recognize that if we do not show love to one another the world has a right to question whether Christianity is true.

A commitment to the Great Commandment calls for us to be student friendly in our educational delivery systems and service oriented in our dealings with faculty, staff, alumni, and other constituencies. At the heart of this commitment is the visible demonstration of valuing one another. We want to model the love and forgiveness of Christ. We will seek to recognize achievement, to reward and applaud success, and to learn together from our failures. We will even search for ways to enhance the rare quality of community, seeking to withstand the pressures of individualism and constantly focusing on an attitude of service and graciousness to all people. There are several implications of these truths.

First, faculty and students at Christian colleges and universities should be better teachers and learners because our motivation for learning is different. We want to learn more about God and His world, His purpose, and His activities as they impact our areas of focus. The purpose of learning is different. It is shaped by values different from just wanting to get a good job, as important as that is.

Second, education that integrates faith and learning, that establishes and shapes a Christian worldview, can help restore lost moral accountability. It can help us be better people, better citizens, and better employees. It gives us standards and ideals at which we can aim in order to be better people because it is an education concerned not only with content but with character as well. Then we can know what is right and do what is right. So a Christian worldview not only impacts and shapes the mind but the will as well.

Education shaped by a Christian worldview can better prepare someone for his or her vocation. This is not mere career preparation, but it helps each of us see that our own unique vocation is a calling from God, a holy thing from God.

The goal is to enable men and women to be prepared for their chosen vocation in order to be salt and light in the marketplace. We want to help students become servant leaders and change agents in our world. The goal is to help us be prepared for work and to see work from God's perspective in a way that will bring glory to Him—preparation for vocation—

not just job training or careers but work, calling, *vocatio*. In our next chapter we will see the implications of these commitments for serving church and society.

Sources

Beaty, Michael, J. Todd Burns, and Larry Lyon. "Faith and Knowledge in American Higher Education." *Journal of the Conference on Faith and History* 29 (1997): 73–81.

Blomberg, Craig. *Matthew*. New American Commentary. Nashville: Broadman & Holman, 1992.

Bok, Derek. *The President's Report, 1986–87, Harvard University.*

Burtchaell, James Turnstead. *The Dying of the Light*. Grand Rapids: Eerdmans, 1998.

Calvin, John. *Institutes of the Christian Religion*. Edited by John T. McNeil. Translated by Ford Lewis Battles. Philadelphia: Westminister, 1960.

Carson, D. A. *The Gagging of God*. Grand Rapids: Zondervan, 1995.

Chandler, Russell. *Racing Toward 2001*. Grand Rapids: Zondervan, 1992.

Damrosch, David. *We Scholars: Changing the Culture of the University*. Cambridge: Harvard University Press, 1995.

Dovre, Paul J. *The Future of Religious Colleges*. Grand Rapids: Eerdmans, 2002.

Eliot, T. S. *Christianity and Culture*. New York: Harcourt Brace, 1940.

Erickson, Millard J. *The Evangelical Heart and Mind*. Grand Rapids: Baker, 1993.

Garber, Steven. *The Fabric of Faithfulness*. Downers Grove: InterVarsity, 1996.

Henry, Douglas V., and Bob Agee, eds. *Faithful Learning and the Christian Scholarly Vocation*. Grand Rapids: Eerdmans, 2003.

Holmes, Arthur F. *All Truth Is God's Truth*. Downers Grove: InterVarsity, 1977.

Hunter, James Davidson. *Evangelicalism: The Coming Generation*. Chicago: University of Chicago Press, 1987.

Huntington, Samuel P. *The Clash of Civilizations and the Remaking of World Order*. New York: Simon & Schuster, 1996.

Justin Martyr. *The First and Second Apologies*. Translated by Leslie William Bernard. Ancient Christian Writers. Mahwah, NJ: Paulist, 1997.

Kerr, Clark. *The Uses of the University*. Cambridge: Harvard University Press, 1995.

Knight, George R. *Philosophy and Education*. Berrien Springs, MI: Andrews University Press, 1989.

Litfin, Duane. *Conceiving the Christian College*. Grand Rapids: Eerdmans, 2004.

Lockerbie, D. Bruce. *A Passion for Learning*. Chicago: Moody, 1994.

McGrath, Alister. *Christianity's Dangerous Idea: The Origins and Transformation of Protestantism, 1500–2000*. San Francisco: Harper San Francisco, 2007.

Marsden, George M. *The Outrageous Idea of Christian Scholarship*. Oxford: Oxford University Press, 1997.

_____. *The Soul of the American University*. Oxford: Oxford University Press, 1994.

Moreland, J. P. *Love God with All Your Mind*. Colorado Springs: NavPress, 1997.

Newman, John Henry. *The Idea of a University*. Notre Dame: University of Notre Dame Press, 1982 [1873].

Noll, Mark A. *The Scandal of the Evangelical Mind*. Grand Rapids: Eerdmans, 1995.

Poe, Harry L. *Christianity in the Academy*. Grand Rapids: Baker, 2004.

_____. *The Gospel and Its Meaning*. Grand Rapids: Zondervan, 1996.

Postman, Neil. *Amusing Ourselves to Death*. New York: Penguin, 1986.

_____. *Technopoly: The Surrender of Culture to Technology*. New York: Vintage, 1993.

Readings, Bill. *The University in Ruins*. Cambridge: Harvard University Press, 1996.

Ringenberg, William C. *The Christian College: A History of Protestant Higher Education in America*. Grand Rapids: Baker, 2005.

Schaeffer, Francis. *The Church before the Watching World*. Downers Grove: InterVarsity, 1971.

Schmeltekopf, Donald D., and Dianna M. Vitanza, *The Future of Baptist Higher Education*. Waco: Baylor University Press, 2006.

Schwenn, Mark. *Exiles from Eden: Religion and the Academic Vocation in America*. New York: Oxford University Press, 1993.

Sloan, Douglas. *Faith and Knowledge: Mainline Protestantism and American Higher Education*. Louisville: Westminister/John Knox, 1994.

Solomon, David. "What Baylor and Notre Dame Can Learn from Each Other." *New Oxford Review* (December 1995): 8–19.

Stott, John R. W. *The Contemporary Christian*. Downers Grove: InterVarsity, 1992.

Waterman, Robert, and Tom Peters. *In Search of Excellence*. New York: Warner Books, 1982.

Wells, David F. *God in the Wasteland*. Grand Rapids: Eerdmans, 1993.

imaginatively—preparing them for leadership and preparing them for life.

Some might question the usefulness of the liberal arts for the twenty-first century technical world. Yet no less a figure than Pope John Paul II urged universities to "stress the priority of the ethical over the technical" and "the primacy of persons over things." Certainly we want graduates to be technologically competent. Yet we know that technology cannot solve all our problems. Echoing Neil Postman, Arthur Holmes notes that from a biblical perspective the claim that technology can solve all our problems is heretical, even idolatrous. Clearly a technological society needs the broad understanding and wisdom of the liberal arts and the Christian Scriptures because they are essential for the thinking and decision making a technological society needs, as well as for giving substance to a Christian worldview.

Building on Holmes's comments, we maintain that the liberal arts also facilitate understanding and effective communication across generations and cultures while providing a common body of knowledge that remains open-ended. This body of knowledge broadens horizons and deepens understanding.

The liberal arts are excellent preparation for professional studies or careers because they educate the person, providing transferable skills and a knowledge of the disciplines on which professions and businesses are built. The liberal arts then do not point just to the life of the artist or the scientist, the scholar or the minister, or even that of the educator or business leader. The liberal arts point toward all of human life.

The Christian liberal arts do not attempt to create a syncretistic understanding between Christian faith and liberal learning. Following Augustine's approach, *credo ut inte* faith is recognized as a precondition of understanding, of genuine knowledge rather than a capstone to a body of knowledge already acquired. We certainly acknowledge that salvific faith is possible without the liberal arts, but the deeper things of the faith needed to shape a full-orbed Christian worldview can only be comprehended with such broad learning.

James Orr, in *The Christian View of God and the World*, maintains that there is a definite view of things, which has a character, coherence, and unity of its own, and stands in sharp contrast with countertheories and speculation. A Christian worldview is not built on two types of truth (religious and philosophical or scientific) but on a universal principle and all-embracing system that shapes religion, natural and social sciences, law, history, health care, the arts, the humanities, and all disciplines of study with application for all of life.

This means that Christ-centered higher education cannot be content to display its Christian foundations merely with chapel services and required Bible classes. We must bring students to a mature reflection of what the Christian faith means for every field of study. In doing so we can help develop a grace-filled convictional community of learning.

Character Development and Service

The purpose of Christian higher education is not only to impart information but also to develop character and competence for effective service. In this endeavor we cannot ignore an emphasis on the moral and spiritual formation and care of the soul. Will Willimon, former dean of the chapel at Duke University, contends for what he refers to as small communities on campuses where students find identity and become accountable. Steven Garber similarly suggests a threefold approach for Christian higher education that includes:

- *Convictions* (developing a worldview sufficient for life's questions and crises);
- *Character* (involving incarnating this worldview); and
- *Community* (living out this worldview in company with mutually committed and stimulating people).

Holistic learning communities are needed where academics, student life, residential life, and campus ministries can work together.

Medieval and Reformation thinkers linked disciplined exploration with moral self-scrutiny in preparation for contemplating and serving God. And it remains the case today that moral, intellectual, and faith development are interconnected in a life integrated by love for God. Christian university faculties need to set the content, objectives, methods, and results of their research within the framework of a coherent worldview that will help develop a Christian spirit of service to others.

Caring, Grace-Filled Community

On this foundational framework grace-filled communities will become a reality—communities that emphasize love, joy, peace, patience, kindness, goodness, faithfulness, gentleness, and self-control as the virtues needed to create a caring Christian context where undergraduate and graduate education, grounded in the conviction that all truth has its source in God, can be offered. Arthur Holmes suggests that for this kind of community to develop, spiritual formation must be intentional, that it depends in large measure on the caring mentor, whether a faculty or staff member, who befriends students, who takes interest in their spiritual life as well as their social and extracurricular activities, who sees benefits to be derived and stumbling blocks to be avoided and advises accordingly, who recognizes a student's gifts, strengths, and weaknesses, who models work as service (and even as a calling from God) and understands that who we are takes priority over what we do.

Building that kind of context—a community of faith and character, a supportive learning community that models appropriate virtues, especially the virtues of grace and love—is a noble goal. We can learn from Dietrich Bonhoeffer, who reflected that we must meet others as the person that he or she is in Christ's eyes. Spiritual love, Bonhoeffer said, recognizes the true image of the other person which he or she has received from Jesus Christ—the image that Jesus Christ Himself embodied and would stamp upon all men and women.

Shared Mission and Core Values

Such a community characterizes the distinctive identity of Christian universities, which are built on the core values of Christ-centered excellence, a focus and priority on people, a connection to the church, and a vision for the future.

A recognition of our identity (who we are) precedes an understanding of our mission (what we are called to do). It is one thing to understand our identity; it is another thing to put it into practice, to find our course and follow it. An outstanding example of a person who followed his course was William

Wilberforce. Wilberforce served as a member of the English Parliament in the late eighteenth century. He had become a Christian through the influence of some of John Wesley's early disciples. His Christian beliefs infused him with a sense of personal purpose, and he seized it. Wilberforce found his mission in life sparked by his outrage over slave trade.

His efforts to end slave trade began in 1787. Year after year his efforts in Parliament were defeated. Decades later, when Wilberforce was on his deathbed, slavery itself was abolished throughout the British Empire.

Individually, we all have a unique purpose and mission to fulfill. Corporately, the mission of Christian higher education involves providing Christ-centered higher education that promotes excellence and character development in service to church and society.

Renewing Minds: The Central Calling of Christ-Centered Higher Education

Our ultimate task, to provide Christ-centered higher education, will be fulfilled as our minds are renewed by God's Spirit. We must become persons whose thinking is shaped by Scripture, by a Christian worldview as we think about subject matter across the curriculum. Please do not hear this call for the renewal of our minds in Christ-centered higher education necessarily as a call for more required courses in Bible in the core curriculum. The goal of Christian universities is *not* to become a Bible college. We respect those institutions who are called to be Bible colleges, but that is *not* the purpose or mission of Christian colleges and universities.

either do we approach subject matter with so-called
ty." We need an effective response to secularized
...nking, one that denies the Enlightenment ideal of autonomous reason and recalls Augustine's model of "faith
seeking understanding." We need to start from the vantage
point of faith in order to integrate our faith with learning
across the curriculum, even as we struggle with issues and
carry on debate in the pursuit of truth. In doing so, following the admonition of the apostle Paul, we will seek to "take
captive every thought to make it obedient to Christ" (2 Cor
10:5 NIV). Such a lofty calling can only be fulfilled across
our learning communities as our minds are renewed by God's
Spirit (Rom 12:2).

Some might fear such an approach to education, thinking that it represents a kind of closed-mindedness. But that is
not the heritage of the best of Christian thinking as exemplified in the Alexandrian or Antiochene schools in the fourth
century, with Augustine, Bernard, or Thomas Aquinas in the
medieval period, or even with Erasmus or Luther in the sixteenth century. Indeed, such an approach is intentionally and
unashamedly Christian; but it recognizes the place of serious
debate and engagement, of testing hypotheses and considering challenges, of changing one's viewpoint or developing
new syntheses. A Christian university, similar to other institutions of higher learning, provides a context for the contest
of ideas.

A serious commitment to the renewing of minds values
exploration and struggle while wrestling with the great ideas
of history and the significant issues of our day, but it does not
apologize for doing so with faith commitments or presuppositions. Within our confessional context and with a sensitivity

to denominational constituencies, we must value intellectual and academic freedom. Within our unity of purpose and the framework of our common mission we can and should expect a range of viewpoints in our thinking. We thus need simultaneously a renewing of our minds to discover and expound God's truth wherever it is found, and an accompanying humility that acknowledges that God, the source of all truth, knows all things and we do not.

Renewing Minds by Promoting Excellence and Developing Character

As Christian universities become intentional about this common mission, they must do so with a commitment to excellence and the holistic development of persons. They will seek to develop a community that is joyously able to contemplate a wide range of things while also seeking to restore the endangered virtues of kindness, humility, love, grace, truth, beauty, goodness, honor, justice, and purity (Phil 2:1–4; 4:8). Excellence, not mere compliance, is the lofty goal of teaching, research, and service. This motivation to excellence is not a matter of pride but a desire to do all things for God's glory because He cares about the quality of work and wants to be involved and reflected in everything that takes place on Christian college campuses. The goal is to pursue excellence without arrogance, to build universities of significance without institutional hubris.

This commitment to excellence particularly has application to the classroom but is equally true in student life, in the business office, on the athletic court or field, in computing services, in facilities and housekeeping, in campus ministries—literally all across our campuses and communities. Perhaps better said, it means Christian colleges will act with faithfulness in everything they do.

Some might ask, "Why would an academic institution see its mission as serving the church, the universal body of Christ?" Others might be equally puzzled as to why a church-related, Christ-centered institution would understand its mission in light of service to society? I believe insights from the apostle Paul might help us understand how this crucial issue of serving both church and society impacts our institutional mission.

Citizens of Two Worlds: Serving Church and Society

A common theme in the writings of the apostle Paul is the dual citizenship of God's people who belong to two worlds, both heaven and earth. Paul developed this idea from his own background and status. In Acts 21–22, we find Paul on the grounds of the temple. He had been taken into custody by a Roman commander. When allowed to address the crowd, Paul claimed that he came from Tarsus, "not just any old city." When the apostle was facing the threat of being scourged, he immediately informed the commander that he was a Roman citizen. Paul was indeed a "high status" citizen, both a Jew from Tarsus and a Roman citizen. This factor was a major advantage, not a disadvantage, for the apostle. In his letter to the Philippians, Paul appeals to this framework when he exhorts the church to strive together, to focus on their shared mission; for after all as Christ-followers they are citizens of "high status," citizens of heaven and earth (Phil 1:27; 3:20).

Because they are citizens of heaven living on earth, Paul exhorts them toward a single purpose, a common mission. He recognizes there is joy among believers when they work together toward a shared goal. The apostle calls on them as men and women who hold dual citizenship in heaven and on earth to live in ways faithful to their citizenship in both places.

Sometimes we get the emphasis of our dual citizenship out of balance. Perhaps you have heard someone say about another person, "He is so heavenly minded that he is of no earthly good." I certainly understand that kind of sentiment, but I'd like to reflect on this a little further.

C. S. Lewis reminds us that a continual looking forward to the eternal world is not, as some modern people think, a form of escapism or wishful thinking but one of the things a Christian is meant to do. It does not mean that we are to leave the present world as it is. If you read history, you will find that the Christians who did most for the present world were just those who thought most of the next. Since Christians have largely ceased to think of the other world, they have become so ineffective in this one. Lewis concludes, aim at heaven and you will get earth "thrown in"; aim at earth and you will get neither.

How should we understand the relationship between this world and the next? Or to put it another way, what is the relationship of culture to Christianity or of society to the church? Or framed even more specifically for us, what is the relationship of the academy to the kingdom of God? These complex questions are at the heart of the identity and mission of Christian universities. On the one hand, as Christians we are a part of this world, of culture, of society; and as those involved in higher education, we are a part of the academy. On the other hand, as Christians we are called to be a distinct new people of God who view life from an eternal perspective.

H. Richard Niebuhr, a widely heralded scholar at Yale University in the middle of the twentieth century, offered some answers to these challenges in a book titled *Christ and Culture* (1951). While the models we will explore do not exactly match his proposals, I believe we can build from his work. I would like to identify at least four ways to think about these issues as they impact the work of Christian higher education, identifying what we do *not* mean as well as what we do mean when we say Christian universities serve church and society.

Church above Society

The first model, which can be called Church above Society, has historically been the viewpoint of the Roman Catholic Church (at least during the Constantinian era and into the Middle Ages) and seems to me to be the model of some portions of the so-called "theonomists" in our times. This view begins with the right starting point, namely that Jesus Christ is King of kings and Lord of lords. But then it makes a huge (and in my opinion wrongheaded) leap that suggests because Jesus Christ is sovereign over all aspects of society that the church as Christ's representative is also sovereign over this world.

Such a view, which was dominant in medieval times, is precisely the view of those Christians today who want to reclaim America by establishing godliness through legislation. When we suggest that Christian higher education exists to serve church and society, this model is *not* what we have in mind. Certainly we want to influence our world toward godliness, including the means of legislation where possible and appropriate, but more so through prayer and persuasion rather than worldly power.

Church apart from Society

The second model, which can be called Church apart from Society, is that of the monastics of the early church and of the Anabaptists of the sixteenth century. Faced with what was viewed as a hopelessly corrupt society, the monastics retreated into the desert, trying to get as far away from their corrupt world system as possible. To be fair, we owe the preservation of most ancient literature to these monks, who copied and so saved these texts.

A millennium later, the Anabaptists confessed in their shared confession (the Schleitheim Confession) of 1527: "We agree . . . a separation shall be made from the evil and from the wickedness which the devil planted in the world."

This perspective, which calls the church out of the culture, was generally the view of many Christians during most of the twentieth century. While as Christians we are not to love the world or the things in the world (1 John 2:15), nor are we to be conformed to this world (Rom 12:2), this second model, which tends more toward isolation than biblical separation, is not what we mean when we suggest that our identity involves engaging the culture by thinking Christianly.

It seems that this second model underestimates the value of this world's culture and government since through common grace unbelievers are able to pursue truth, create objects of beauty, launch worthwhile social projects, and participate in society with integrity and skill. It likewise fails to recognize that God's people also participate in the fall by having a fallen, deceptive, and sinful nature. So even when we participate in society with the intention of doing good, we must acknowledge that we do not have all the answers. With appropriate humility we acknowledge that those outside the church have important insights and skills to offer, often better than our own. Thus in a Christian liberal arts university, we certainly want to study texts and ideas more broadly based than just those produced by Christian authors.

Church beneath Society

Though the first two views are at opposite ends of the spectrum, they do share a common commitment to the uniqueness of Christianity. A decade after Niebuhr's work in this area, a third model developed, which suggests that Christianity is not unique in this world, even implying that the church needs to be influenced by the world. Such a view, which can be called Church beneath Society, has often been identified with Harvard professor Harvey Cox in his book *The Secular City*. Similar ideas are often prevalent in those places where the secularization of the church is well under way.

Those who have adopted this position have exchanged the ancient wisdom of the church, embodied in the Scriptures, for the world's wisdom. In its secularized form it is often suggested that a relationship with Jesus Christ might be helpful, but it is not believed to be necessary since people are not really sinful but basically good.

When we describe institutions like Union University, where I serve, as a Christ-centered institution that is evangelical by conviction and Baptist by tradition, rigorously academic and unashamedly Christian, we are distancing ourselves from this third option.

Church and Society

Our final position best explains what is meant when we claim that Christian universities serve both church *and* society because we believe that God is sovereign over church *and* society. As Christians we belong to both spheres. We must avoid the tendency to confuse church *and* society on the one hand or divorce them on the other. We are not called to rule over the world (at least in this age) but to relate to it and to seek to influence it for good within the framework of a Christian worldview.

Thus we can and should gladly encourage students to pursue any and all morally upright vocations (if indeed that is their calling from God, without seeing any as a second-rate vocation) as a work where they can serve God and others. This can happen not by escaping culture or identifying with it but by engaging it through Christian thinking and Christlike service, with the goal of influencing it ultimately for God's glory.

This approach not only magnifies the doctrine of redemption but also the doctrine of creation by suggesting that God as Creator is sovereign over all that has been made. We thus call for a responsible realism: responsible to be in the world and to work responsibly in it, seeking to engage and influence the world, while realistic about the truth that this world is not all there is. In fact this world will remain sinful, affected by the fall until the restoration of all things. During this time while we wait for the restoration of all things, especially as we study those areas most closely related to society at large—economics, philosophy, political science, ethics, sociology, psychology, social work, nursing, biology, to name a few—we must remember that we are followers of Christ arrayed in truth serving a world impacted by sin, and thus the issues are sometimes messy and the answers murky, as even now we see through a glass dimly.

Thus in the tradition of the apostle Paul, Augustine, and the Reformers, we are suggesting that we live in two worlds: the academy and kingdom of God, the society and the church. Yet it is imperative for us to recognize that as those called to the work of Christian higher education, we are citizens of God's kingdom in the academy and agents of the church in society.

Our goal is to influence society in a redemptive way without imposing our viewpoint through worldly power. We do so in the world of higher education by participating in the academy as Christian scholars; and, as George Marsden and others have exhorted us, we must do so without an inferiority complex.

 We do not believe that our primary responsibility and focus as educators is to denounce the fallen ways of culture though we do believe that one way we engage society is through God-centered cultural analysis. Yet I believe we need to concentrate our efforts on a more constructive approach, focusing on ways that we can with excellence produce quality art, outstanding literature, great music, and respectable scholarship grounded in the liberal arts tradition while developing servant leaders who as change agents can manifest what it means to be salt and light in our society.

Likewise we must prepare students to perform with competence and skill in the world—especially those called to the professions of health care, education, business, law, social work, and engineering—preparing at both the undergraduate and graduate levels. As we do so, we will encourage and enable young men and women to grow intellectually, socially, and spiritually so that they can become leaders in society, in homes, in communities, and in the church. Christian universities can give leadership to the church by providing scholarship that will enable the Christian public to make good decisions about issues they face in their personal lives and in society, thus becoming significant resources where Christian leaders can turn to find direction regarding the challenges facing both the church and our contemporary society.

A Call to Mission-Driven Service

Our mission then at this time is to live out this high calling for *this* generation. The Bible records the essence of a mission-driven life in the epitaph for King David. Acts 13:36 simply says, "David had served God's purpose in his own generation." Wouldn't it be wonderful if history could say the same for those who serve Christian universities at this moment in time. Thus we want to invite students, staff, faculty, administrators, and trustees alike to join together as we seek to live out faithfully the implications of this distinctive identity and mission.

Following the exhortation of the apostle Paul, we pray that we will strive together with one mind (Phil 1:27), with renewed minds (Rom 12:2), focused on a common mission, assured of a distinctive identity grounded in shared values, committing ourselves afresh to serve both church and society with excellence in the high calling of Christ-centered higher education. We now turn our attention to think more clearly about the importance of a Christian worldview as foundational to this high calling.

Sources

Augustine. *The City of God*. In *A Select Library of the Nicene and Post-Nicene Fathers of the Christian Church*. Edited by Philip Schaff. Grand Rapids: Eerdmans, 1977.

Belmonte, Kevin. *William Wilberforce: Hero for Humanity*. Grand Rapids: Zondervan, 2007.

Benne, Robert. *Quality with Soul*. Grand Rapids: Eerdmans, 2001.

Boice, James Montgomery. *Mind Renewal in a Mindless Age*. Grand Rapids: Baker, 1993.

_____. *Two Cities, Two Loves*. Downers Grove: InterVarsity, 1996.

Bonhoeffer, Dietrich. *Life Together*. Translated by John W. Doberstein. New York: Harper, 1954.

Burtchaell, James T. *The Dying of the Light*. Grand Rapids: Eerdmans, 1998.

Carnell, E. J. *An Introduction to Christian Apologetics*. Grand Rapids: Eerdmans, 1948.

Carson, D. A. *Telling the Truth*. Grand Rapids: Zondervan, 2000.

Carter, Stephen L. *The Culture of Disbelief*. San Francisco: Basic, 1993.

Cox, Harvey. *The Secular City: Secularization and Urbanization in Theological Perspective*. New York: Macmillan, 1965.

Cranfield, C. E. B. *A Critical and Exegetical Commentary on the Epistle to the Romans*. 2 vols. Edinburgh: T&T Clark, 1975–79.

Dernick, Christopher. *Escape from Scepticism: Liberal Education as if Truth Mattered*. LaSalle, IL: Sherwood Sugden & Co., 1977.

Diekema, Anthony J. *Academic Freedom and Christian Scholarship*. Grand Rapids: Eerdmans, 2000.

Dockery, David S. *Our Christian Hope*. Nashville: LifeWay, 1998.

Dwight, Benjamin W. *The Higher Christian Education*. New York: Barnes & Burr, 1860.

Eliot, T. S. *Christianity and Culture*. New York: Harcourt Brace, 1940.

Elshtain, Jean Bethke. "Beyond Traditionalism and Progressivism, or Against Hardening of the Categories." *Theology Today* 58 (April 2001) 4–13.

Garber, Steven. *The Fabric of Faithfulness: Weaving Together Belief and Behavior during the University Years*. Downers Grove: InterVarsity, 1996.

Gleason, Philip. *Contending with Modernity: Catholic Higher Education in the Twentieth Century*. New York: Oxford University Press, 1995.

Godwin, Gail. *Evensong*. New York: Ballantine, 1999.

Gushee, David P. "The Christian University." Unpublished Lectures, Palm Beach Atlantic University, 2001.

Hauerwas, Stanley, and John H. Westerhoff, ed. *"Holy Experiments" in Higher Education*. Grand Rapids: Eerdmans, 1992.

Henry, Carl F. H. "Baptists and Higher Education." In *Baptists Why and Why Not Revisited*. Edited by T. George and D. George. Nashville: Broadman & Holman, 1997.

Hoekema, David. *Campus Rules and Moral Community: In Place of In Loco Parentis*. Lanham, MD: Rowman and Littlefield, 1994.

Holmes, Arthur. *Building the Academy*. Grand Rapids, MI: Eerdmans, 2001.

_____. *Shaping Character: Moral Education in a Christian College*. Grand Rapids: Eerdmans, 1990.

Hunsberger, George R. and Craig Van Gelder. *The Church between Gospel and Culture*. Grand Rapids: Eerdmans, 1999.

Hunter, James Davison. *Culture Wars: The Struggle to Define America*. New York: Basic, 1991.

_____. *The Death of Character: Moral Education in an Age without Good or Evil*. New York: Basic, 2000.

Kuyper, Abraham. "Lectures on Calvinism." Stone Lectures. Princeton University, 1898.

Lewis, C. S. *Mere Christianity*. New York: Macmillan, 1955.

MacIntyre, Alasdair. *Three Rival Versions of Moral Inquiry*. Notre Dame: University of Notre Dame Press, 1990.

Marsden, George. *The Outrageous Idea of Christian Scholarship*. New York: Oxford University Press, 1997.

Melick, Richard R., Jr. *Philippians, Colossians, Philemon*. New American Commentary. Nashville: Broadman & Holman, 1991.

Moberly, Sir Walter. *The Crisis in the University*. London: SCM, 1949.

Nash, Arnold. *The University and the Modern World: An Essay in the Social Philosophy of University Education*. London: SCM, 1945.

Newman, John Henry. *The Idea of a University.* Notre Dame: University of Notre Dame Press, 1982 [1873].

Niebuhr, H. Richard. *Christ and Culture.* New York: Harper, 1951.

On Catholic Universities: Ex Corde Ecclesiae. U. S. Catholic Conference, 1990.

Orr, James. *The Christian View of God and the World.* Grand Rapids: Eerdmans, 1948 [1901].

Polhill, John B. *Paul and His Letters.* Nashville: Broadman & Holman, 1999.

Postman, Neil. *Technopoly: The Surrender of Culture to Technology.* New York: Vintage, 1993.

Sloan, Douglas. *Faith and Knowledge: Mainline Protestantism and American Higher Education.* Louisville: Westminster John Knox, 1994.

Stott, John R. W. *Guard the Truth.* Downers Grove: InterVarsity, 1996.

Tanner, Kathryn. "The Religious Significance of Christian Engagement in the Culture Wars." *Theology Today* 58:1 (April 2001): 28–43.

Weigel, George. *Witness to Hope: The Biography of Pope John Paul II.* New York: HarperCollins, 1999.

Wilkens, Steve, and Alan G. Padgett. *Christianity and Western Thought.* Vol. 2, *Faith and Reason in the 19th Century.* Downers Grove: InterVarsity, 2000.

Willimon, William, and Thomas Naylor. *The Abandoned Generation: Rethinking Higher Education.* Grand Rapids: Eerdmans, 1995.

Wolfe, Alan. "The Opening of the Evangelical Mind." *Atlantic Monthly*, October 2000, 55–76.

Wuthnow, Robert. *The Restructuring of American Religion.* Princeton: Princeton University Press, 1988.

3

Shaping a Christian Worldview

*"Teaching everyone with all wisdom, so that
we may present everyone mature in Christ."*

Colossians 1:28

*"There is not one square inch in the whole domain
of our human existence over which Christ, who
is sovereign over all, does not cry: 'Mine!'"*

Abraham Kuyper, 1898 Stone
Lectures, Princeton University

*"In an age when university learning has lost a cohesive
center—in terms of an unchanging God and fixed moral
values—evangelical campuses have the grand opportunity of
exhibiting the comprehensive unity of truth and indispensable
importance of mind, conscience, godliness and love."*

Carl F. H. Henry,
"Worldview of a Theologian"

*"It is the Christian view of things in general which is
attacked, and it is by an exposition and vindication
of the Christian view of things as a whole that
the attack can most successfully be met."*

James Orr, *The Christian View
of God and the World*

One of our local newspapers recently published a series of articles focusing on the rise of crime in our region. Each author addressed the crime issue from the standpoint and perspective of economic deprivation. After reading the articles, I thought I must be missing something. One approach was anthropological, another sociological, another economic—each dealing with systemic issues, which I do not doubt for a moment exist. But missing from the articles was any sense of responsibility. Crime was discussed without raising the issue of morality. I could not believe it. Then it dawned on me that diverse worldviews were at work.

Everyone Has a Worldview

A Chinese proverb says, "If you want to know what water is, don't ask the fish." Water is the sum and substance of the world in which the fish is immersed. The fish may not reflect on its own environment until suddenly it is thrust onto dry land, where it struggles for life. Then it realizes that water provided its sustenance.

Immersed in our environment, we have failed to take seriously the ramifications of a secular worldview. Sociologist and social watchdog Daniel Yankelovich defines *culture* as an effort to provide a coherent set of answers to the existential situations that confront human beings in the passage of their lives. A genuine cultural shift is one that makes a decisive break with the shared meaning of the past. The break particularly affects those meanings that relate to the deepest questions of the purpose and nature of human life. What is at stake is how we understand the world in which we live. The issues are worldview issues.

Christians everywhere recognize that there is a great spiritual battle raging for the hearts and minds of men and women around the globe. We now find ourselves in a cosmic struggle between a morally indifferent culture and Christian truth. Thus we need to shape a Christian worldview and life view that will help us learn to think Christianly and live out the truth of Christian faith.

The reality is that everyone has a worldview. Some worldviews are incoherent, being merely a smorgasbord of ideas from natural, supernatural, premodern, modern, and postmodern options. An examined and thoughtful worldview, however, is more than a private personal viewpoint; it is a comprehensive life system that seeks to answer the basic questions of life. A Christian worldview is not just one's personal faith expression, nor is it simply a theory. It is an all–consuming way of life, applicable to all spheres of life.

Distinguishing a Christian Worldview

James Orr, in *The Christian View of God and the World*, maintains that there is a definite Christian view of things which has a character, coherence, and unity of its own and stands in sharp contrast to counter theories and speculations. A Christian worldview has the stamp of reason and reality and can stand the tests of both history and experience. Such a holistic approach offers a stability of thought, a unity of comprehensive insight which bears not only on the religious sphere but on the whole of thought. A Christian worldview is not built on various types of truth (religious and philosophical or scientific) but on a universal principle and all–embracing system that shapes religion, natural and social sciences, law, history, health care, the arts, the humanities, and all disciplines of study with application for all of life.

James Orr in 1891 and Abraham Kuyper in 1898 brilliantly articulated a Christian worldview at the turn of the nineteenth century. James Sire, C. S. Lewis, Carl F. H. Henry, J. P. Moreland, William Lane Craig, Arthur Holmes, David Nagle, and Charles Colson, among others, have articulated well the essence of a Christian worldview. Now we must seek to build upon their work to articulate a Christian worldview for the twenty–first century, with all of its accompanying challenges and changes, and to show how such Christian thinking is applicable across the educational curriculum.

At the heart of these challenges and changes, we see that truth, morality, and interpretive frameworks are being ignored if not rejected. Such challenges are formidable indeed. Throughout modern culture the very existence of normative truth is being challenged.

We observe these challenges in the poststructuralism of Jean–François Lyotard, the deconstructionism of Jacques Derridá, the radical subjectivism of Michael Foucault, and the reader–focused hermeneutic of Stanley Fish. The influence of these philosophical shifts can be observed in popular culture as exemplified in the lyrics of country music artists like Diamond Rio, who sing that "it's all interpretation, if you want to know the truth, you have to read between the lines." A normative view of truth has been devalued, if not lost, in our contemporary culture.

As we have seen in our initial chapters, we must hear afresh the words of Jesus from what is called the Great Commandment (Matt 22:36–40) to be able to respond to these challenges. Here we are told not only to love God with our whole hearts and souls but with our minds as well. Jesus' words refer to a wholehearted devotion to God with every aspect of our being from whatever angle we choose to consider it—emotionally, volitionally, or cognitively. This kind of love for God results in taking every thought captive to make it obedient to Christ (2 Cor 10:5), a wholehearted devotion to distinctively Christian thinking. This means being able to see life from a Christian vantage point; it means thinking with the mind of Christ.

The beginning point for building a Christian worldview is a confession that we believe in God the Father, Maker of heaven and earth (the Apostles' Creed). We recognize that "in Him all things hold together" (Col 1:15–18 NIV), for all true knowledge flows from the One Creator to His one creation.

A worldview must seek to answer questions like:

- Where did we come from?
- Who are we?
- What has gone wrong with the world?
- What solution can be offered to deal with these challenges?

In addition, a worldview must seek to answer the key questions of life and their general implications or specific applications such as: Why do we exist? What is the purpose of life? To these foundational questions and attending issues we now turn our attention.

We Believe in God, Maker of Heaven and Earth: A Worldview Starting Point

A worldview must offer a way to live that is consistent with reality by presenting a comprehensive understanding of all areas of life and thought in every aspect of creation. The starting point for a Christian worldview brings us into the presence of God without delay. The central affirmation of Scripture is not only that there is a God but also that God has acted and spoken in history. God is Lord and King over this world, ruling all things for His own glory, displaying His perfections in all that He does in order that humans and angels may worship and adore Him. God is Triune; there are within the Godhead three persons: Father, Son, and Holy Spirit.

To think wrongly about God is idolatry (Ps 50:21). Thinking rightly about God leads to eternal life (John 17:3) and should be the believer's life objective (Jer 9:23–24). We can think rightly about God because He is knowable (1 Cor 2:11), yet we must remain mindful that He is simultaneously incomprehensible (Rom 11:33–36). God can be known, but He cannot be completely known (Deut 29:29).

God is personal and differentiated from other beings, from nature, and from the universe. In contrast, other worldviews say that God is in a part of the world, creating a continual process. The process itself, it is claimed, is God—or becoming God. Yet Scripture affirms that God is self–existent, dependent on nothing external to Himself. He is infinite, meaning that God is not only unlimited but that nothing outside God can limit God. He is infinite in relation to time (eternal), in relation to knowledge (omniscient), and in relation to power (omnipotent). He is sovereign and unchanging. God is infinite and personal, transcendent and immanent. He is holy, righteous, just, good, true, faithful, loving, gracious, and merciful.

Without the use of any preexisting material, God brought into being everything that is. Both the opening verse of the Bible and the initial sentence of the Apostles' Creed confess God as Creator. Creation reveals God (Ps 19) and brings glory to Him (Isa 43:7). All of creation was originally good but is now imperfect because of the entrance of sin and its effects on creation (Gen 3:16–19). This is, however, only a temporary imperfection (Rom 8:19–22), for creation will be redeemed in the final work of God, the new creation.

The Creator God is not different from the God who provides redemption in Jesus Christ through His Holy Spirit. Creation itself is the work of the Trinitarian God. God is the source of all things. This means that God has brought the world into existence out of nothing through a purposeful act of His free will. A Christian worldview affirms that God is the sovereign and almighty Lord of all existence. Such an affirmation rejects any form of dualism—that matter has eternally existed, or that matter must, therefore, be evil since it is in principle opposed to God, the source of all good.

Furthermore, a Christian worldview contends that God is set apart from and transcends His creation. It also maintains that God is a purposeful God who creates in freedom. In creation and in God's provision and preservation for creation, He is working out His ultimate purposes for humanity and the world. This affirms the overall unity and intelligibility of the universe. In this unity we see God's greatness, goodness, and wisdom.

Who Are We? Where Did We Come From?

God has created us in His image and likeness (see Gen 1:27). At first this might appear to refer to our physical make-up, meaning that we look like God. This physical resemblance is not what the Bible means by the terms *image* and *likeness* of God.

We must be cautious in our thinking so as not to imagine the image of God as only some aspect in men and women but to see that humans are *in* the image of God. By "in the image" we mean that nothing in us is separable, distinct, or discoverable as the divine image. Each person individually and the entire race corporately are the image of God, but no single aspect of human nature or behavior or thought patterns can be isolated as the image of God. Since men and women have been created in the image of God, they are the highest forms of God's earthly creation. All other aspects of creation are for the purposes of serving men and women and are thus anthropocentric, or human centered. Yet humans have been created to serve God and are theocentric, or God centered. Thus a Christian worldview helps us fulfill our responsibility for God–centered thinking and living.

What Has Gone Wrong with the World?

The entrance of sin into the world has had great and negative influences on God's creation, especially on humans created in God's image. As a result of sin, the image of God, though not lost, is severely tarnished and marred. The role of exercising dominion (see Gen 1:28) has been drastically limited by the effects of sin on humans and the course of nature. The ability to live in right relationship with God, with others, with nature, and with our own selves has been corrupted. Ultimately all are spiritually dead and alienated from God (see Eph 2:1–3). This does not mean that we are all as bad as we can be but that not any of us are as good as we should be. We are therefore unable to reflect properly the divine image and likeness (see Rom 1:18–32).

It is important to see that the fall into sin (see Gen 3) was not just a moral lapse but also a deliberate turning away from God and rejection of Him. The day Adam and Eve disobeyed God they died spiritually, which ultimately brought physical death (see Gen 2:17). Sin's entrance has caused a sinful nature in all humanity. Therefore men and women are not simply sinners because they sin, but they sin because they are sinners. People thus think and act in accordance with their fallen natures.

This idea of a sinful nature is most significant when reflecting on our relationship to God. Because of the entrance of sin into the world and our inheritance of Adam's sinful nature (see Rom 5:12–19), we are by nature hostile to God and estranged from Him (see Rom 8:7; Eph 2:1–3). We have wills that do not obey, eyes that do not see, and ears that do not hear because spiritually we are dead to God.

While we function as free moral agents with free wills, our decisions and actions are always affected by sin. In seeking to understand what has gone wrong with the world, we recognize that human choices are negatively influenced by sin. In regard to our relationship with God, we do not genuinely repent or turn to God without divine enablement because we are by nature hostile to God.

Any articulation of a Christian worldview must wrestle with the problem of sin. The result of sin (what theologians call depravity) refers to the fact that all aspects of our being, including our thinking and emotions, are negatively influenced. People still do right and good things as viewed by society, but these thoughts and actions, no matter how noble or benevolent, fall short of God's glory (Rom 3:23). We can affirm that people choose to do good, but a Christian worldview helps us distinguish between the good and the ultimate good, which is the goal of pleasing God.

Attributing the blame for problems in our world to our sinful nature does not mean that all people are totally corrupt. Factors such as environment, emotional makeup, heritage, and the continuing effect of our creation in the image of God influence or limit the degree of our corruption. Yet a Christian worldview recognizes that all types of immoral actions, whether lying, murder, adultery, power–seeking, homosexuality, pride, or failing to love one another are related to our alienation from God. All in this world are estranged from God. The good news is that our sin was judged at the cross of Jesus Christ. He has regained what was lost in Adam (Rom 5:12–21). The grace of God has provided restoration for believers and has brought about a right relationship with God, with one another, with nature, and with ourselves.

What Solution Can Be Offered?

At the core of a Christian worldview is the foundational truth that Jesus Christ's life and death exemplified divine love and exerted an influence for good and sacrifice. More importantly, Christ's death provided for sinners like you and me a sinless sacrifice that satisfied divine justice. This incomprehensibly valuable sacrifice delivered sinners from their alienation and reconciled and restored sinners from estrangement to full fellowship and inheritance in the household of God.

Christ's work on the cross provided two major benefits for mankind. First, it atoned for our sins (Rom 3:25; 1 John 2:2; 4:10; Heb 2:17). Second, Jesus Christ has broken the power of sin, guilt, death, and Satan, bringing about a people who have been bought with a price (see Col 2:15; 1 Pet 1:8–19).

But with that atonement also came redemption. Jesus' work on the cross has made it possible for those who have been redeemed in Him to be reconciled by placing their faith in Him. Believers in Christ no longer stand under God's judgment. Jesus' reconciling work involves bringing humanity out of alienation into a state of peace and harmony with God. Our separation and brokenness created by sin has been healed in Christ. Believers have been delivered from estrangement to fellowship with God who now accepts and treats them as children rather than as transgressors (see 2 Cor 5:18–20; Eph 2:12–16; Col 1:20–22).

Central to this Christian worldview message is the resurrection of Jesus Christ (see 1 Cor 15:3–4). The resurrection establishes Jesus' lordship and deity, as well as guarantees the salvation of sinners (see Rom 1:3–4; 4:24–25). Jesus' resurrection enables believers to see, think, and live anew.

General Implications of a Christian Worldview

A Christian worldview becomes a driving force in life, giving us a sense of God's plan and purpose for this world. Our identity is shaped by this worldview. We no longer see ourselves as alienated sinners. A Christian worldview is not escapism but an energizing motivation for godly and faithful thinking and living in the here-and-now. It also gives us confidence and hope for the future. In the midst of life's challenges and struggles, a Christian worldview helps to stabilize life, serving as an anchor to link us to God's faithfulness and steadfastness.

Thus a Christian worldview provides a framework for ethical thinking. We recognize that humans, who are made in God's image, are essentially moral beings. We also recognize that the fullest embodiment of good, love, holiness, grace, and truth is in Jesus Christ (see John 1:14–18).

A Christian worldview has implications for understanding history. We see that history is not cyclical or random. Rather, we see history as linear, a meaningful sequence of events leading to the fulfillment of God's purposes for humanity (see Eph 1). Human history will climax where it began—on the earth. This truth is another distinctive of Christian thinking, for Christianity is historical at its heart. According to its essential teaching, God has acted decisively in history, revealing Himself in specific acts and events. Moreover, God will act to bring history to its providential destiny and planned conclusion.

God who has acted in history in past events will also act in the future to consummate this age. So when we ask, "How will it end?" we do not simply or suddenly pass out of the realm of history into a never–never land. We pass to that which is nevertheless certain of occurring because God is behind it and is Himself the One who tells us it will come to pass.

Developing a Christian worldview is an ever–advancing process for us in which Christian convictions more and more shape our participation in culture. This disciplined, vigorous, and unending process will help shape how we assess culture and our place in it. Otherwise, culture will shape us and our thinking. Thus a Christian worldview offers a different way of thinking, seeing, and doing, based on a new way of being.

A Christian worldview is a coherent way of seeing life. It is a perspective distinct from such philosophies and approaches as deism, naturalism, and materialism (whether Darwinistic, humanistic, or Marxist forms), existentialism, polytheism, pantheism, mysticism, or deconstructionist postmodernism. The theistic emphasis of Christianity provides bearings and direction when confronted with New Age spirituality or secularistic and pluralistic approaches to truth and morality. Fear about the future, suffering, disease, and poverty are informed by a Christian worldview grounded in the redemptive work of Christ and the grandeur of God. As opposed to meaningless and purposeless nihilistic perspectives, a Christian worldview offers meaning and purpose for all aspects of life.

Particular Applications

While many examples could be offered, we will offer five particular applications that have relevance on a contemporary university campus where a Christian worldview will provide the difference in perspective.

1. *Sexuality* has become a major topic for those entering the third millennium. Much confusion exists among Christians and non–Christians. Sexuality is good in the covenant relationship of mutual self–giving marriage. Outside the covenant marriage both heterosexual and homosexual relations are sinful and have a distorted meaning, a self–serving purpose, and negative consequences.

2. Another pressing issue of our day is *environmental concerns*. Environmental stewardship means we have a responsibility to the nonhuman aspects of God's creation. Since God's plan of redemption includes His earthly creation as well as human (see Rom 8:18–27), we should do all we can to live in it carefully and lovingly.

3. A third area important in our culture includes *the arts and recreation*. The arts and recreation are understood as legitimate and important parts of human creativity and community. They express what it means to be created in the image of God. We need to develop critical skills of analysis and evaluation so that we are informed, intentional, and reflective about what we create, see, and do.

4. For almost two centuries *science* has been at the forefront of our modern world. We must explore how we see scientific issues from the vantage point of a Christian worldview. An understanding of God includes the knowledge we gain through scientific investigation. With the lens of faith in place, a picture of God's world emerges where science and faith can be viewed as complementary.

5. An understanding of *the value of work* is important for any culture. Work is a gift from God and is to be pursued with excellence for God's glory. We recognize that all honest professions are honorable, that the gifts and abilities we have for our vocation (*vocatio*/calling) come from God, and that prosperity and promotions are gifts from God.

Toward Christian Thinking in Higher Education

As we move further into the twenty–first century, there are inescapable choices to be made; and these choices have great implications for all aspects of life, particularly for higher education. Those who teach and study in Christ–centered institutions should take to heart the words of the apostle Paul: "Do not be conformed to this age, but be transformed by the renewing of your mind" (Rom 12:2).

Our task will be intellectually challenging. The work is not easy, but it is faithful to the calling upon Christ–followers. There is no room for anti-intellectualism in Christian higher education. We are to have the mind of Christ, a concept that certainly requires us to think and wrestle with the challenging ideas of history and the issues of our day. To do otherwise would result in another generation of God's people becoming ill–equipped for faithful thinking and service in this still–new century. A Christian worldview is needed to help interpret an ever–changing culture. Instead of allowing our thoughts to be captivated by culture, we must take every thought captive to Jesus Christ.

A Call to Intentional Christian Higher Education

A call to intentional Christian higher education is a call to "take captive every thought to make it obedient to Christ" (2 Cor 10:5 NIV). Paul's words call us toward a wholehearted devotion to Christ—not just with our hearts but with our minds as well. It is a call to think Christianly. We need more than just novel ideas and new delivery systems; we need distinctively Christian thinking. Or as previously noted, we need "to think in Christian categories." This means being able to see life and learning from a Christian vantage point; it means thinking with the mind of Christ.

4

Reclaiming the Christian Intellectual Tradition

"Stand firm and hold to the traditions you were taught."

2 Thessalonians 2:15

*"All that is meant by tradition, then,
is the faithful handing down
from generation to generation of scripture
interpretation consensually received worldwide
and cross-culturally through two millennia."*

Thomas C. Oden, *The Rebirth of Orthodoxy*

*"Truth is, in Christian teaching, both universal and
universally longed for. . . . So, whoever sincerely pursues
truth, existentially as well as in the scholarly disciplines,
seeks—and thereby honors the God who is Truth."*

Robert P. George, *The Clash of Orthodoxies*

*"Reason itself is a matter of faith. It is an act of faith to
assert that our thoughts have any relation to reality at all."*

G. K. Chesterton, *Orthodoxy*

O ur vision for systemic Christian colleges and universities is not just about an inward, subjective, personal, and pious Christianity. That would miss the distinctive mission to which we have been called. We must recognize that the Christian faith impacts how we live, how we think, how we write books, how we govern society, how we treat one another. The Christian faith is more than a recipe for eternal life and happiness in this world.

That being the case, it is our responsibility today as students, staff, faculty, and administrators to ask how the Christian faith impacts what we do on our campuses on a day-to-day basis. How does the Christian faith impact our understanding of language? of narrative? of truth? of history? of government? of justice? of beauty? of art? of our work? We believe that God is calling Christian colleges and universities to help move the faith of many Christians out of the intellectual ghetto. Certainly the kind of antiintellectual, personal, inward, and subjective faith we see around us in such popular forms of Christianity is not representative of what can be called the great Christian intellectual tradition.

At the heart of our calling is the challenge to engage the culture, to prepare a generation of leaders who can step up to the plate in the academy, in our community, in government, in health care, in society, and in the church. The breadth and depth of the Christian intellectual tradition must be reclaimed, revitalized, renewed, and revived for us to carry forth this vision.

Reclaiming the Christian Intellectual Tradition: Clement of Alexandria as a Guide

Let us explore together the early shape of the Christian intellectual tradition as exemplified in one of the first great Christian scholars, Clement of Alexandria, and then reflect on the implications of his thinking for us in the twenty-first century. As we explore the priorities and opportunities of the future, it will be helpful to look back eighteen hundred years to this brilliant scholar who serves as a helpful model for our time.

Intellectual Leader in Early Christianity

Titus Flavius Clement, who lived from about AD 150 to the time of his martyrdom around AD 215, is best known as Clement of Alexandria. He is considered by many to be the first great Christian scholar. Clement became the leader of the Alexandrian School in AD 190, a position he held until after the turn of the century when persecution forced him out of Egypt into Cappadocia.

His principal literary works produced during this time were a trilogy titled the *Exhortations*, the *Tutor*, and the *Miscellanies*. The three works follow a pattern in which, according to Clement, the divine logos first of all converts us (which is the focus of the *Exhortations*), then disciplines us (which is the focus of the *Tutor*), and finally instructs us (which is the focus of his rather unsystematic work titled the *Miscellanies*).

Guide for Our Context

Clement serves as an instructive guide for us in our context because of his wide range of learning, his love of philosophy and literature, his concern for the cultivation of an intellectually serious Christianity, his interaction with the issues and trends in the changing world of his day, and perhaps most importantly because he was a layperson—which is the case for more than 90 percent of faculty and staff, as well as students at most Christian colleges and universities. Many of the great thinkers in the early years of Christianity were ordained bishops and elders in the church. The fact that Clement was a layperson is all the more significant for us in our context today.

Clement's overarching concern was to develop a view of the world and of life from the standpoint of wisdom in which he could engage the various strands of thought and culture in his day. We cannot underestimate Clement's impact as a pioneer of serious Christian thought. Even though his writing is at times unsystematic, he nevertheless presents a coherent and consistent explication of the importance of Christian thinking and ethics for the challenges of his day.

Learning from the Past

For the most part Clement's reflections are philosophical, ethical, and even political rather than theological; yet his works are grounded in the divine logos, the Word of God who was incarnate in Jesus Christ. Just as Clement looked to the past in drawing from Moses, Israel's great leader, from Plato, the great philosopher, and from Philo, the Jewish philosopher who preceded him in Alexandria, so we today can look to Clement as a source and guide for the challenges of our day. Clement was a master at making full use of the philosophy of his day without compromising his polemical analysis of pagan culture.

His works reflect great understanding of Plato and Aristotle. His political exposition, with its various subdivisions, is treated as a science and organized into an ambitious and complex scheme that maps out all the sciences and their specialties under the broad headings of natural, physical, and theoretical science. Yet there is a difference between Clement and the great Greek philosophers. Whereas the Greek philosophical tradition was always implicitly constructive in its articulation of political leadership, Clement was concerned to speak of philosophical kingship as something already present because God has undertaken it and manifested it in His Son. Thus the discussion of human kingship or political leadership was for him a worldview issue rather than a constructive discussion. Clement was a master at showing how the political order as we experience it in history falls short of the sovereign rule of the divine Word.

Singular Source for Liberal Arts Thinking: Great Teacher

Clement's work also delves into issues of economics, business, the management of wealth, concern for the poor, and social issues of his time. He truly was a Renaissance person prior to the Renaissance, a singular source for liberal arts thinking. But ultimately Clement was an educator, and this again is what gives so many who are concerned about Christian higher education a connection with this giant of the early third century. He understood quite seriously his calling as a teacher, and thus his favorite self-designation was *paidagogos*, the title of his middle work, which we know as the *Tutor*.

Engagement with Non-Christian Ideas

Clement also had a great appreciation for the art and music of his day and used it in his persuasive appeal for the Christian faith to those in the early third century. His writings refer to Christ as the noblest minstrel while observing that the harp and lyre are men and women. Christ draws music from human hearts by the Holy Spirit; indeed, Christ is Himself the new canticle, whose melody subdues the fiercest and hardest natures.

Clement showed the transcendence of Christianity and contrasted it with the vilest paganism of his day and the hopelessness of pagan poetry and philosophers. Ultimately Clement pointed to the source of all life in God by maintaining that men and women are born for God. Full or ultimate truth, Clement claimed, is found in Christ alone.

Importance of the Alexandrian Context

As we make these observations about the significance of Clement's thought, it is important to recognize the context in which he worked. Alexandria was a great city which served as the center of culture and trade in Egypt. A great university was developed there. The intellectual temper was broad and tolerant, and it became in many ways an intercultural city where many races mingled. The great eclectic intellectual movements of the day were represented. And Plato was the most favored of all the old masters. Neoplatonism, the philosophy of the pagan renaissance, had a strong foothold in Alexandria, which was also one of the chief seats of the pagan/Christian amalgamation known as Gnosticism. The leading Gnostic heretics Basillides and Valentinus taught there. It is no surprise, therefore, to find that Christians were impacted by this eclectic *zeitgeist*.

In this context Clement thrived and became one of the greatest and most admired Christian teachers by the end of the second century. His important works were written after AD 190, and his work known as the *Miscellanies* was not completed until near the time of his death, though most of it was written between 200 and 210.

Indeed the *Miscellanies* seemingly wander at random from time to time as Clement moves about from subject to subject. He began with the importance of philosophy and the pursuit of Christian knowledge. He then defended his own scientific interests. Next he showed how faith is related to knowledge and emphasized the superiority of God's revelation to human philosophy.

Yet for Clement it was vitally important to recognize that God's truth is found in both special revelation and general revelation or philosophy. Thus he maintained that it is the duty of the Christian to neglect neither. Likewise, the study of doctrine and science, drawn from a similar twofold source, served to instruct the believers. Clearly Clement understood the importance of serious Christian intellectual engagement. Though Clement did not always get it right, and at times sounds more Platonic (almost Gnostic) than Christian, he remains in many ways a source and exemplar of the great Christian intellectual tradition that we must seek to carry forth at our Christian institutions.

The Shape of the Christian Intellectual Tradition

Drawing upon the model of Clement of Alexandria, I would like once again to call for the priority of serious Christian thinking on Christian college campuses as the underlying vision to carry us forward, looking back to the early third century to help shape our twenty-first-century world. We must recognize that we can build new buildings, raise significant gifts, recruit great students, create wonderful programs, and design creative delivery systems; but if it is not undergirded by serious Christian thinking, then our vision will be misguided.

we can explore the ideas in history and the issues of our day as they are encountered throughout the curriculum across our campuses.

Knowledge of God and Knowledge of Ourselves: Correlative Not Sequential

The well-known or the twofold knowledge John Calvin used to introduce his famous *Institutes* is applicable for us as well. In the opening line of this classic work, the great sixteenth-century Reformer observed that all understanding we possess proceeds from the knowledge of God and the knowledge of ourselves. This is not a sequential exercise but a correlative one. It is not that we first master theology and then explore all other areas across the curriculum, but it is a bringing together of our knowledge of God and our knowledge of the subject matter under investigation. It is a recognition that we cannot know ourselves or truly know other things without knowing God. And we cannot know God without knowing that we are created in the image of God and that all things being explored fall under the umbrella of God as both Creator of the universe and the Source of all truth.

Without this correlative approach to learning, all knowledge is basically abstract, whether biology, economics, English, engineering, political science, or the arts. As Timothy George says, without this correlative learning we cannot understand the purpose of the things being explored. In George's words, we might understand how things work but not what they are for. We may learn how to clone a baby but not whether we should do it. We may learn to construct an atom bomb but not when, if, or how to use it. We may ingeniously construct a maximum security prison, but without such correlative learning we may not know how to treat the prisoners. We may develop an expert understanding of technology but fail to rec-ognize, in the words of Neil Postman, the tendency to amuse ourselves to death.

Vantage Point of "the Faith"—More Than Theological Affirmation

Certainly we all learn apart from the great Christian intel-lectual tradition, apart from the vantage point of faith. But we cannot connect these things into a unified whole; we can-not fully understand the grand metanarrative; we cannot truly grasp how to explore and engage the issues in history and sci-ence, business and health care, apart from this approach to learning. Thus we must seek to sanctify the secular because Jesus Christ has come to the earth.

We recognize that the confession we make about Him has profound implications for ecology, technology, sexuality, how we understand the world, and how we treat one another. Indeed our confession that Jesus Christ is central to the Christian faith is a counter to the wrongheaded thinking we encounter at every turn whether from Docetists, Gnostics, deists, mys-tics, or the postmodern antirealists of our day. Against these various interpretations of God and the world, the incarnation of Christ stands as a challenge. This essential theological af-firmation of the incarnation has implications for all things across the curriculum.

Implications for the University Curriculum

One clear example of such is the iconoclastic controver-sy of the eighth century summarized in the Second Nicene Council of 787. Here the church reaffirmed with the first Nicene Confession that Jesus was fully human and truly physical and thus could be painted. This central affirmation had implication for the arts and for understanding this world. It recognized that a Christian icon was not an idol but an image of the Image. Thus, in many ways the case for Christian art finds its foundation in the Second Nicene Council.

Art, Drama, Music, Literature

The implications for the authenticity of all other subject matter are likewise inherently present in this confession, whether it is our understanding of art, drama, music, literature, economics, philosophy, health care, or the sciences. Once again we learn from Timothy George, the Beeson Divinity School dean, who maintains that when learning has become disconnected from this great Christian intellectual tradition the true has devolved into intellectualism, the good into moralism, and the beautiful into mere aestheticism. Thus our responsibility at Christian colleges and universities is to make sure that our confession about Jesus Christ is not marginalized or Gnosticized in our contemporary world. We must resist this temptation with all of our might and underscore our affirmation of the First and Second Nicene Confessions:

> We believe in one Lord, Jesus Christ, the
> only Son of God, eternally begotten of the
> Father, God from God, Light from Light, true
> God from true God, begotten, not made, of one
> Being with the Father. Through Him all things
> were made. For us and our Salvation He came
> down from heaven: by the power of the Holy
> Spirit He became incarnate from the Virgin
> Mary, and was made man.

We can join with Clement of Alexandria and those who have followed him for the last eighteen hundred years in saying that we will seek to sanctify the secular as we carry forth the Christian intellectual tradition in our institutions.

Connectedness across the Curriculum

We believe these commitments have implications even for our curriculum development. Such an understanding of the educational enterprise can enrich the liberal arts experience, with its ideal of educating the whole person. Mark Roche suggests that only in a university where reflection on God or on an absolute understanding of truth can life's most fundamental questions, which are increasingly set aside at secular institutions of higher learning, be addressed. Thus we understand that we study history and the classics in order not simply to learn *about* the past but to learn *from* the past.

Liberal Arts and Professional Programs

From this perspective we employ the quantitative tools of the social sciences not simply as a formal exercise with mathematical models but in order to develop sophisticated responses to pressing and complex social issues like racism, the AIDS crisis, the breakdown of the family, and the challenges in the Sudan. Thus we see that faith and values shape the intellectual inquiry across our campuses. This faith dimension, growing out of our heritage, enriches the liberal arts ideals in ways that even the best liberal arts colleges, apart from this faith commitment, can only approximate—not to mention the impact it has for the professional programs at our campuses.

Strengthen Scholarship

We also see that our faith is not separated from scholarship but rather is fully integrated into it. The Christian faith is not an add-on to learning or something that is done in a separate sphere on the other side of the campus. Certainly such a commitment cannot take place without excellent programs in history, science, philosophy, literature, mathematics, and Christian thought.

Interdisciplinary Connectedness

But more than seeing these departments as stand-alone departments, the best of the Christian intellectual tradition calls for us to think about how these important matters can be integrated in an interdisciplinary way across our campuses. It helps us understand that there is a place for music and the arts because God is the God of creation and beauty. It helps us understand that sociology can make observations to strengthen the family as well as religious structures because we recognize that we are all created in the image of God. It helps us understand that economics can help address problems facing communities and society at large. It helps us understand that political science can strategize about ways to bring justice and peace to our world. Such an educational approach strengthens our commitment to the sciences and to engineering in hope of developing a Christian perspective on the environment.

Indeed, this faith commitment provides the meaningful anchor for synergies of all kinds across the curriculum. Finally, an educational model grounded in the Christian faith that seeks to advance the Christian intellectual tradition cannot forget the importance of application for the lives of people.

Applications for Life

We must recognize that there is no corner of the universe to which the Christian faith is indifferent—not one inch, not one second—and thus a call to sanctify the secular is a recognition of the fullness of the incarnation and the intemporization of Jesus Christ. Thus the Christian faith has significance for all spheres of life.

Love for God Requires a Love for All Humanity: Doers of the Word

We would not want to be interpreted as implying that the intellectual aspect of the faith is all there is to Christianity, no, not at all; yet that's the part of the kingdom for which we have been given responsibility on our campuses and as members of the academy at large. Certainly right thinking is not all there is to the Christian faith; we must apply the Christian faith for the New Testament says we are also to be "doers of the word" (Jas 1:22). That is the second aspect of the Great Commandment that we explored in the opening chapter. We are to love our neighbor and care for orphans and widows.

Agents of Reconciliation

We are to be agents of reconciliation in the church and in society. We are to build bridges where there are walls, particularly with reference to the racial divide that has haunted our country since its inception.

This is what it means to love our neighbor, to be doers of the word. If we stop and think upon that last phrase, it is shocking. We normally are hearers of the word, thinkers about the word. We can spell a word and reflect upon a word, but to *do* the word puts a different shape on what we are all about.

We need to seek God's guidance in how we can best contribute to constructive exercises that will help us honor, respect, and love one another. We want to model the love and forgiveness of Christ in the workplace. We desire to be quick to offer forgiveness when we have been wronged and claim responsibility and seek forgiveness when we have wronged others. We will ask God to help us be agents of reconciliation to a broken and hurting world, which seemingly remains in disorder as a result of the fall. We pray that God would give us grace to be agents of redemption in this broken world and to embrace one another regardless of national, ethnic, or racial background.

Intellectual, Moral, and Character Formation

To the extent we succeed in putting these things into practice and in guiding students in these important matters, we will succeed in the development of the intellectual, moral, and character formation across our campuses. Thus, at the heart of our Christ-centered approach to education is the belief that God has revealed Himself to us in creation, in history, in our conscience, and ultimately in Christ and that this revelation is now primarily available to us in Holy Scripture. It is here we find the words of Jesus Himself, claiming that He alone is the way to God, claiming that He is not only the way and the life, but He is also the truth.

This revealed truth is the foundation of all we believe, teach, and do. We believe that this God-revealed truth is the framework in which we understand and interpret our world, the events of human history as well as our responsibilities toward God and one another in this world. This is what it means for us to advance the Christian intellectual tradition and to love God with our hearts, our strength, and our minds.

Now we must think more reflectively about what it means to integrate this tradition with teaching and learning in our post-Christian culture.

Sources*

Ackroyd, Peter R., and C. F. Evans, eds. *The Cambridge History of the Bible.* Vol. 1, *From Beginnings to Jerome.* Cambridge: Cambridge University Press, 1970.

Avis, Paul, ed. *The History of Christian Theology.* 3 vols. Grand Rapids: Eerdmans, 1986.

Bauer, Walter. *Orthodoxy and Heresy in Earliest Christianity.* Translated and edited by R. Kraft and G. Krodel. Philadelphia: Fortress, 1971.

Bebis, G. S. "Concept of Tradition in the Fathers of the Church." *Greek Orthodox Theological Review* 15 (1970): 22–55.

Bell, Harold Idris. *Cults and Creeds in Graeco–Roman Egypt.* Liverpool: Liverpool University Press, 1954.

Benne, Robert. *Quality with Soul. How Six Premier Colleges and Universities Keep Faith with Their Religious Traditions.* Grand Rapids: Eerdmans, 2001.

Bettensen, Henry, ed. *Documents of the Christian Church.* Oxford: Oxford University Press, 1963.

Bigg, Charles. *The Christian Platonists of Alexandria.* Oxford: Clarendon, 1886.

Book of Common Prayer. New York: Oxford University Press, 1979.

Bray, Gerald. *Creeds, Councils, and Christ.* Downers Grove: InterVarsity, 1984.

I have learned much from, adapted from, and borrowed from several key sources for this chapter, particularly Timothy George and H. E. W. Turner.

Brown, Harold O. J. *Heresies*. Garden City, NY: Doubleday, 1984.

Burtchaell, James T. *The Dying of the Light: The Disengagement of Colleges and Universities from their Christian Churches*. Grand Rapids: Eerdmans, 1998.

Chadwick, Henry. *Early Christian Thought and the Classical Tradition*. Oxford: Clarendon, 1966.

Clement of Alexandria. *Paidagogus; Protrepticus; Stromateis*. In *The Ante-Nicean Fathers*. Edited by Alexander Roberts, James Donaldson, Philip Schaff, and Henry Wace. 10 vols. Grand Rapids: Eerdmans, reprint, 1994.

Dockery, David S. *Biblical Interpretation Then and Now*. Grand Rapids: Baker, 1992.

Ellsperman, C. L. *The Attitude of the Early Christian Fathers Towards Pagan Literature and Learning*. Washington, DC: Catholic University of America, 1949.

George, Timothy. *Theology of the Reformers*. Nashville: Broadman, 1988.

_____. "The Pattern of Christian Truth." *First Things* 154 (2005): 21–25.

Gonzalez, Justo L. *History of Christian Thought*. 3 vols. Nashville: Abingdon, 1970.

Grant, Robert M. *After the New Testament*. Philadelphia: Fortress, 1967.

_____. *Gnosticism and Early Christianity*. New York: Oxford University Press, 1960.

_____. *Greek Apologists of the Second Century*. Philadelphia: Westminster, 1988.

Hatch, Edwin. *The Influence of Greek Ideas and Usages on Christianity*. New York: Harper, 1957.

Holmes, Arthur F. *Building the Christian Academy*. Grand Rapids: Eerdmans, 2001.

_____. *The Soul of the Christian University*. Grand Rapids: Calvin College, 1997.

Kelly, J. N. D. *Early Christian Creeds*. London: Black, 1972.

_____. *Early Christian Doctrine*. New York: Harper & Row, 1960.

Lewy, Hans. *Chaldean Oracles and Theurgy: Mysticism, Magic, and Platonism in the Later Roman Empire*. Paris: Etudes Augustiniennes, 1978.

Lilla, R. C. *Clement of Alexandria: A Study of Christian Platonism and Gnosticism*. London: Oxford University Press, 1971.

Litfin, Duane. *Conceiving the Christian College*. Grand Rapids: Eerdmans, 2004.

Marrou, H. I. *A History of Education in Antiquity*. Translated by George Lamb. New York: Sheed and Ward, 1956.

Marsden, George. *The Soul of the American University: From Protestant Establishment to Established Non-belief*. New York: Oxford University Press, 1994.

McClelland, Joseph. *God the Anonymous: A Study in Alexandrian Philosophical Theology*. Cambridge: Patristic Foundation, 1976.

McCoy, Jerry. "Philosophical Influences on the Doctrines of the Incarnation in Athanasius and Cyril of Alexandria." *Encounter* 38 (1977): 362–91.

McGrath, Alister E. *Historical Theology: An Introduction to the History of Christian Thought*. London: Blackwell, 1998.

Mollard, Elnar. *The Conception of the Gospel in the Alexandrian Theology*. Oslo: Jacob Dybwad, 1938.

Myers, Ken. "The Practice of True Religion." Unpublished Commencement Address. Westminster Theological Seminary, 2002.

Oden, Thomas C. *The Rebirth of Orthodoxy*. San Francisco: Harper & Row, 2003.

O'Donovan, Oliver, and Joan Lockwood O'Donovan. *From Irenaeus to Grotius: A Sourcebook in Christian Political Thought.* Grand Rapids: Eerdmans, 1999.

Osborn, Eric F. *The Philosophy of Clement of Alexandria.* Cambridge: Cambridge University Press, 1975.

Otto, Walter. *The Homeric Gods: The Spiritual Significance of Greek Religion.* London: Thomas & Hudson, 1954.

Pagels, Elaine. *The Gnostic Paul: Gnostic Exegesis of the Pauline Letters.* Philadelphia: Fortress, 1975.

Pelikan, Jaroslav. *The Christian Tradition: A History of the Development of Doctrine.* Vol. 1, *The Emergence of the Catholic Tradition* (100–600). Chicago: University of Chicago Press, 1971.

_____. *The Idea of the University: A Reexamination.* New Haven: Yale University Press, 1992.

Poe, Harry L. *Christianity in the Academy.* Grand Rapids: Baker, 2004.

Postman, Neil. *Amusing Ourselves to Death.* New York: Penguin, 1985.

Richardson, Cyril C., ed. *Alexandrian Christianity.* Philadelphia: Westminster, 1953.

Roche, Mark W. *The Intellectual Appeal of Catholicism and the Idea of a Catholic University.* Notre Dame: University of Notre Dame Press, 2003.

Sandmel, Samuel. *Philo of Alexandria.* New York: Oxford University Press, 1979.

Sellers, R. V. *Two Ancient Christologies: A Study in the Christological Thought of the Schools of Alexandria and Antioch in the Early History of Christian Doctrine*. London: SPCK, 1954.

Sullivan, Robert E. *Higher Learning and Catholic Traditions*. Notre Dame: University of Notre Dame Press, 2001.

Thompson, J. Alexander. "Alexandria." *International Standard Bible Encyclopedia*. Edited by G. W. Bromiley. 4 vols. Grand Rapids: Eerdmans, 1979–1988.

Turner, H. E. W. *The Pattern of Christian Truth: A Study of the Relations Between Orthodoxy and Heresy in the Early Church*. London: Mobray, 1954.

Wagner, Walter. "Another Look at the Literary Problem in Clement of Alexandria's Major Writings." *Church History* 37 (1968): 251–62.

Wolfson, Harry. *The Philosophy of the Church Fathers*. Cambridge, MA: Harvard University Press, 1956.

5

Integrating Faith and Learning

*"Set an example of good works yourself,
with integrity and dignity in your teaching."*

Titus 2:7

*"Truth is so obscure in these times, and falsehood so
established, that unless we love the truth, we cannot know it."*

Blaise Pascal, *Pensées*

*"The evangelical passion for truth must become a passion
for the evangelical mind."*

Alister McGrath, *A Passion for Truth*

*"By an evangelical 'life of the mind' I mean . . . the effort to
think like a Christian—to think within a specifically Christian
framework—across the whole spectrum of modern living."*

Mark A. Noll, *The Scandal
of the Evangelical Mind*

W e live in a pluralistic world in which people are constantly asked to join things together or hold ideas together that in reality do not so belong. Religious or philosophical pluralism maintains that reality is composed of a multiplicity of ultimate beings, principles, or substances. In this view, 2 plus 2 equals 4 and does not necessarily equal 4, which on the face of it is absurd. In that same vein, some argue that a light switch can be on and off at the same time.

I have no intention of making a case for religious pluralism. I do, however, want to suggest that sometimes we who believe in absolute truth are too quick to frame issues as either/or rather than both/and. On first blush, some would tell us that linking authentic Christian commitment with serious academics and genuine scholarship is an antinomy or at best an oxymoron. Yet the motto of the institution where I serve, *religio et eruditio*, issues a clarion call for us not just to tolerantly hold together the ideas of <u>religious commitment and scholarship</u> but <u>to joyfully embrace them.</u>

In the history of the church, heresy has most often raised its ugly head when people have wrongly insisted on either/ or answers. Thus when discussing the Trinitarian God, some have argued incorrectly for modalism (three manifestations of one God) or tritheism (three gods), rather than for the classic Athanasian understanding of the Trinity: three in One and One in three. Rightly understood, we can even point to the Holy Trinity as the supreme model of unity *and* variety. While thinking about the second member of the Trinity, some are prone to repeat the wrongheaded thinking of second-century Ebionites or Docetists by stressing either the humanity or deity of Jesus Christ rather than the historic Chalcedonian confession that Jesus is both truly God and truly human.

Still others, on less central issues such as the coming of the kingdom of God, suggest that the kingdom is either already present or still future rather than recognizing that it is both here and yet to come. These important theological assertions are true because of the "divine and" (a term borrowed from Union University Dean Tom Rosebrough).

The Significance of the Conjunction *And*

As everyone knows, *and*, the translation of the Latin *et*, is the most basic conjunction in the English language. We use conjunctions daily without much thought of their importance unless we are sitting in a grammar class. Then we recognize that there are paratactic, hypotactic, and inferential conjunctions, in addition to causal conjunctions and conjunctions of purpose or result. Perhaps you are more familiar with categories like:

- connectives such as *and,*
- adjunctives like *also,*
- ascensive conjunctions such as *even,*
- adversatives such as *but,* or
- conjunctions of contrast such as *another.*

Conjunctions connect words, clauses, sentences, paragraphs, and larger ideas. Conjunctions "bind together" (*conjungo*). Sometimes we assume the usage of conjunctions and leave them out altogether as a result of our rapidity of thought, a phenomenon which grammarians call "asyndeton." Here I want carefully and intentionally to address the importance of "binding together" at Christian universities by exploring the meaning of the "divine and."

Love for God and Love for Study

A motto like *religio et eruditio* affirms our love for God and our love for study, the importance of devotion and the importance of instruction, the place of piety and the place of scholarship, the priority of affirming and passing on the tradition and the significance of honest intellectual inquiry. These matters are in tension but not in contradiction; and rightly understood, they can be seen as connectives, bound together, and not exclusive categories. We begin with *religio*—a faith commitment that informs *eruditio*, all learning, which in turn shapes expectations for living. The conjunction of faith and learning is the essence of a Christian university; this joint mission defines the distinctive difference in a Christian university education.

The Starting Point

Our thinking must start with the board of trustees. Christian universities must have a board of trustees composed entirely of Christians—men *and* women, clergy *and* laypeople—whose primary task is to attend to the Christian character of the institution. Trustees certainly have responsibility for all financial aspects of a university, but their fiduciary responsibility equally includes concern for the overall mission of the university. They must oversee matters of both Christian truth and financial responsibility. They must encourage faithful

99

stewardship in annual budget matters while simultaneously charting a vision for the future.

The trustees will do this primarily but not exclusively by appointing to the major leadership positions of an institution persons who are actively committed to the ideal of a Christian university. Without this kind of vision and commitment from the board of trustees, an institution will not become an intentional or systemic Christian university.

As James Burtchaell in *Dying of the Light* has so accurately and insightfully recognized, being a faithful Christian university will involve much more than mere piety. History shows that a commitment to piety alone will not sustain the ideal of a Christian university. As we observed in our previous chapter, the Christian intellectual tradition calls for rigorous Christian thinking in all areas, as historically exemplified in the writings of Clement, as well as Origen, Augustine, Aquinas, Bernard of Clairvaux, Erasmus, Luther, Calvin, Pascal, Jonathan Edwards, Dorothy Sayers, C. S. Lewis, and other contemporary thinkers. A school or department of Christian studies must play a central role in carrying on this tradition by offering courses required of all students in both biblical studies and the various areas of Christian thought.

Such courses are not merely exercises in spiritual devotion or professional preparation, as important as these tasks may be, but they provide the foundation for serious intellectual wrestling with literary, philosophical, scientific, technological, and worldview issues.

The core curriculum establishes the beginning framework for the uni[ty] in a Christian university. This framework refers to the constitutive belief that the world proceeded from a Creator by intelligent design and in that sense is a unified whole. While this approach does not address every question, it nevertheless begins with the confession of the Apostles' Creed: "I believe in God the Father Almighty, Maker of Heaven and Earth." This constitutive belief informs the entire curriculum about the beginning point of a Christian worldview over against rival metaphysical and epistemological views. The affirmation of God as Creator is as significant for a Christian worldview and life view as is the tenet of God as Redeemer.

Certainly this important premise, similar to the exclusive claim that salvation is found only in Christ, is controversial, even countercultural in today's world. Thus, part of the mission of the Christian university must be a quest for unity, a unified understanding of knowledge. Such exploration involves finding ways of seeing and knowing what sometimes, in a mysterious and yet undiscovered sense, is already there. As Johannes Kepler (1571–1630), the man famous for discovering that the orbits of the planets are not circles but ellipses, said, "The chief aim of all investigations of the external world should be to discover the harmony imposed on it by God" (cited by Colson and Pearcey).

All faculty members at a Christian university today, like Johannes Kepler in the seventeenth century, have the privilege of being sustained by this conviction and the responsibility to pass on the Christian intellectual tradition as it informs and impacts all the various disciplines. We believe such a responsibility to teach, inform, and communicate these traditions is possible because all human beings, everywhere and at all times, are made in the image of God. We believe this universality of humankind makes possible both teaching and learning.

Contrary to trends in today's higher education world, a Christian viewpoint contends that a species-centered discourse should not be replaced by an ethno-centered discourse which is characteristic of most postmodern thought and lies at the root of what is often called multiculturalism. The latter approach refers only to the views of a particular group or community rather than to what truly holds universally for humans everywhere at all times.

Even an ethnocentric philosopher like Richard Rorty recognizes the implications for the belief that humans are created in God's image. He acknowledges that the Christian tradition contains certain universalist ideals—ideals that Rorty claims are still "gratefully invoked by free-loading atheists" like himself (*Objectivity, Relativism, and Truth,* 202).

Because we can think, relate, and communicate in understandable ways, and since we are created in the image of God, we can creatively teach, learn, explore, and conduct research. A Christian university, in common with any other institution of higher learning, must surely subordinate all other endeavors to the improvement of the mind in pursuit of truth. Yet a focus on the mastery of content, though primary, is not enough. We believe that character and competency development are equally important. Furthermore, we think the pursuit of truth is best undertaken within a community of learning that also attends to the moral, spiritual, and social development of its students, following the pattern of Jesus, who Himself increased in wisdom and stature and in favor with God and humankind (Luke 2:52).

The moral and spiritual virtues have vital cognitive significance and hence strengthen both teaching and learning. Thus we believe that humility strengthens and arrogance hampers the learning process. Not only humility but faith, love, gratitude, and other virtues are essential for a full-orbed approach to Christian higher education.

Certainly this makes a difference in how we relate to colleagues, students, and other scholars and even in the way we interact with and evaluate their ideas. The unity of knowledge, shaped by love, is informing and foundational for all scholarship, teaching, and learning. From this foundation comes our commitment to faith and learning, to both knowledge *and* virtue, throughout the curriculum. These commitments shape our appreciation for the foundational role of the liberal arts in the Christian university.

The Foundation of Liberal Arts Education

Cardinal Newman, in his classic work *The Idea of a University*, articulated the strongest argument found anywhere that the study of the liberal arts is good for its own sake, a viewpoint with which many educators at least sympathize. Yet Newman's idealism at this point was seriously challenged in the nineteenth century. And the twenty-first-century world, for which current students are preparing, certainly differs from Cardinal Newman's world. Most Americans who pursue higher education do so primarily to prepare themselves for work, and many who pursue the liberal arts do so to prepare themselves for a future in the academy or in one of the learned professions such as law, medicine, or ministry.

Building on Cardinal Newman's assertions, we contend that students should pursue a liberal arts-based education because it is foundational to true learning and quality living.

We believe it is good in itself *and* yet good for something else, to serve and edify others. Thus the classic understanding of work, *vocatio*, in the Christian tradition as a social situation where human beings use their God-given talents and acquired knowledge and preparation to serve others enables us to define professional preparation.

This view of work is to be distinguished from mere vocationalism. As Dorothy Sayers correctly notes, in nothing have Christians so lost their hold on reality as in their failure to understand and respect the secular vocation. We have, she maintains, allowed work and religion to become separate departments. We have forgotten that the secular vocation can itself be sacred. We sometimes tend to extend this separation by thinking of the liberal arts and professional preparation as unrelated spheres. Yet I believe we can define, shape, and embrace professional education in health care, education, human and social services, and the business world, not as something adjunctive to, and certainly not in contrast to, but as connected to the strong liberal arts tradition at Christian universities.

We foremost must equip students to think and to understand the world through the foundation established by the liberal arts and the core curriculum. Yet we are simultaneously challenged to prepare them well for their concurrent callings. Education should not be perceived as a set of impossible choices between the study of the classic disciplines or service to society. We must creatively and integratively develop ways for the "divine and" to find a balance between the liberal arts and professional preparation while encouraging excellence within all of these fields of endeavor. This balance, like excellence and achievement in any area of life, is possible only by the grace of God.

Light *and* Life: Carrying on the Tradition

Thus we are challenged to carry on the classic liberal arts tradition while shaping a faithful model of Christian higher education for a new century. Our challenge is faithfully to preserve and pass on the Christian tradition while encouraging honest intellectual inquiry. I believe these can coexist, even if in tension, in an enriching dialectical interdependence.

So our choice is not an unquestioning acceptance of either tradition or open-ended inquiry. The unquestioning acceptance of tradition can degenerate into traditionalism. On the other hand, free inquiry, unanchored to faith and tradition, often results in unbelieving skepticism, advancing the directionless state that characterizes so much of higher education today. Such an approach cannot sustain the Christian tradition and its truth claims. Neither of these approaches represents our vision for a Christian university.

Christian universities are called to reflect the life of Christ and to shine the light of truth. Our unique calling is not to be forced into inappropriate either/or choices but to be appropriately both/and. We reject those who call for us to create false dichotomies or join together unrelated ideas in an irrationalistic pluralistic fashion. Instead we commit ourselves to the "divine and" grounded in Jesus Christ Himself, who is both fully God and fully human and who is for us both light and life.

The Apostle Paul as Model

As we think further about this important theme, we turn to the apostle Paul for guidance. Paul arrived in Athens (Acts 17:16–31) to encounter the culture of his day, which we might define as a highly educated and sophisticated pre-Christian culture.

Athens was the cradle of democracy, the foremost of the city-states at the height of the Grecian Empire (fifth to third centuries BC). By the time Paul visited Athens, the city was no longer a leading military or political power. Yet the cultural influence of Athens remained unsurpassed. The city's contributions in sculpture, literature, philosophy, and rhetoric were unparalleled. Athens still carried the distinction of being the native city of Socrates (470–399 BC) and Plato (427–347 BC) and the adopted home of Aristotle (384–322 BC) and Zeno (335–263 BC).

Cicero (106–43 BC) observed that in spite of its decline in political power, Athens still enjoyed great renown. Though Greece had weakened, its reputation was still supported by the influence of Athens. As commentators like John Stott and John Polhill have observed, there is something enthralling about Paul in Athens, the great Christian apostle amid the glories of ancient Greece. Though times had changed, Athens still had an unrivaled reputation as the Roman Empire's intellectual center.

Paul, while waiting for Timothy and Silas to join him in Athens, became a keen observer as he walked around to see the sights of the city. Even today when one travels to Athens, the Parthenon and other architectural remains, though in partial ruin, have a special splendor for any first-time visitor, as was my own experience on a recent visit.

Paul was no uneducated or uncultured visitor. He had been blessed with a massive intellect and graduated from the prestigious institutions of his day in Tarsus and Jerusalem. No doubt he valued and appreciated the city's impressive history, art, architecture, literature, and wisdom. Yet it was not these things that grabbed his attention. He was distressed to see that the city was literally "smothered under a forest of idols" (Acts 17:16). More gods were worshipped in Athens than in all the rest of the country. The Roman satirist who claimed that it was easier to find a god in Athens than a person was hardly exaggerating. Innumerable temples, shrines, altars, and statues could be found, some so large they could be seen from forty miles away. Paul was not blind to their beauty, but he was grieved that they did not honor the one true God, the Father of the Lord Jesus Christ.

The cultural trends that shape much of our world today are similarly influenced by the rise of neopaganism and the various and diverse forms of spirituality. Thus we believe Paul can become an insightful guide to enable us to respond to this changing post-Christian world in which we live and work.

Paul's Approach

We find it fascinating that Paul was able to proclaim the greatness of God not only in the religious places (the synagogue) and the marketplaces (Acts 17:17) but also in the center of the intellectual world (Acts 17:19). We would certainly expect the apostle Paul to be comfortable proclaiming the greatness of God in the synagogue, and we are not surprised that he moves easily into the marketplace. But to take the concept of the grandeur of God into the Areopagus, the intellectual center of the city, might be surprising to some. This is no surprise, however, to those who recognize that Paul saw all of life from a God-centered perspective. Listen to him reflect on God's greatness in Romans 11:33–36:

> Oh, the depths of the riches of the wisdom
> and knowledge of God!
> How unsearchable his judgments, and his
> paths beyond tracing out! . . .
> For from him and through him and to him are
> all things.
> To him be the glory forever! (NIV).

Similarly, it should not surprise anyone to learn that the greatness of God is faithfully proclaimed in chapel programs on Christian university campuses. It probably would surprise few that the greatness of God is often proclaimed in campus activities, whether in a campus ministry event, a mission trip, or a conversation following a late-night dorm Bible study. But what about the other places on campus, particularly the classroom? Should we expect to find references to the greatness of God in the heart of the intellectual center of our campuses? We believe the answer is yes, and Paul's address to the intellectual leaders in Athens contains five key themes which can be applied to the integration of faith and learning on Christian college campuses.

First, *God is the Creator of the universe* (Acts 17:24). This view was quite different from the pantheism of the Stoics or the world of chance of the Epicureans. So too Paul was different from those today who would deny that God is both the personal Creator of everything that is and the personal Lord over all He has made. It is absurd to think that the One who spoke creation into being and holds it together by the word of His power (Col 1:15–17; Heb 1:2–3) can be housed in shrines built by human hands (Acts 17:24).

Yet Christians often trivialize God by not recognizing His grandeur and His greatness. In a prominent issue of *First Things*, we find a quote from Charles Misner, professor emeritus of physics at the University of Maryland, talking about Albert Einstein. Misner, himself a noted scientist, said:

> I do see the design of the universe as essentially a religious question, that is one should have some kind of respect and awe for the whole business. Its very magnificence should not be taken for granted. In fact that is why I think Einstein had so little use for organized religion, although he strikes me basically as a very religious man. Einstein must have looked at what the Christians said about God and felt that they were blaspheming. He had seen much more majesty than they had ever imagined, and they were just not talking about the real thing. (*First Things*, December 1991, 63.)

Einstein died in 1955, and since then Christians have only continued to trivialize God. Donald McCullough, in his work *The Trivialization of God*, has suggested that we run the risk of creating a manageable deity by turning God into some divine self-help recipe. Einstein was saying that secular scientists have seen more of the grandeur of God in the world of God than most Christians have seen in the Word of God. Do we have a proper respect for the Creator God? Do we have a superficial view of God and the world?

Paul could proclaim the grandeur of God as Creator because he was amazed at the magnitude of creation. And today we know far more about this creation than those in Athens ever imagined. Scientists know that light travels 5.87 trillion miles a year, what is referred to as a light year. Our galaxy is about 100 million light years across, which means that our galaxy is about 587 million trillion miles across. Within the optical range of our best available telescopes today, about one million such galaxies have been discovered. And in our galaxy there are about 100 billion stars, with our sun being one of the smaller ones. Our sun is about 6000 degrees Centigrade on the cooler surface, and it travels about 155 miles per second through the galaxy. It will complete one revolution in two hundred million years. When we study these things and recognize that there is a personal God who spoke this world into being and holds it by the word of His power (Col 1:15–17; Heb 1:2), should there not be a response of awe at the grandeur of God?

Paul's second point is that *God is the providential sustainer of all life.* God is not the one who needs to be sustained, but He is the one who gives life and breath to everyone and everything else (Acts 17:25). So we declare not our independence from God but our dependence on God. We recognize that He does not depend on us but we on Him.

Third, *Paul says that God is the ruler of all nations* (Acts 17:26); and fourth, he is *the Father of all human beings* (Acts 17:26–28) by virtue of His role as Creator. Thus we are all created in His image and can respond to Him and relate to one another. We can think, reason, love, worship, and communicate because we are created in His image. Paul explains these things by an appeal to God's truth made known in God's general revelation of nature, human experience, and history.

In redemptive terms God is the Father of *only those who are in Christ*, and we are His children only by redemption and grace. Yet in creation terms, God is the Father of all humankind, and all are His creatures, depending on Him for life. In addressing these key themes about God, Paul strategically quoted from Greek philosophers and poets to expose his listeners' inconsistency. Thus he brought the Christian faith to bear on their own thought patterns.

This strategy of integrating faith and knowledge then is at the heart of intentional Christian higher education viewed from the vantage point of the grandeur of God. Paul understood cultural categories of the time and used them to express the reality of divine revelation. He had obviously studied and learned the philosophical and literary matters of his day and was able to use them as building blocks in his communication. Paul demonstrated an appreciation of Athenian culture and was able to bring truth to bear on the prevailing *zeitgeist* of that culture.

The key aspect of Paul's strategy involved the integration of his Christian faith with those cultural issues that allowed him to adjust the cultural assumptions of that pre-Christian context in light of God's eternal truth. He accomplished this integration particularly through his understanding of God as a transcendent, creating, sustaining, and self-disclosing God who has made humans in His image. Finally, *He provided evidence of coming judgment*, which will take place because of God's ultimate manifestation of Himself through the resurrected Christ (Acts 17:31).

Toward a Model of Faith and Learning for a Post-Christian Context

You might ask what these events from two thousand years ago have to do with education at Christian universities in the early years of the twenty-first century. We would contend that we can learn much from Paul's approach. As Paul understood his culture, so must we seek to understand our own. By demonstrating an understanding of our contemporary post-Christian culture, we are then able to engage that culture through the arts, the sciences, engineering, social sciences, the humanities, the worlds of business and education, as well as health care issues with a measure of credibility. Therefore, Paul's words to the three groups identified in Acts 17 enable us to see that the Christian faith is to be made known in places of worship, in the marketplace, and yes, even in the academy and intellectual centers.

The essence of the Christian faith is that God is Savior, but we fail to understand the comprehensiveness of the Christian faith unless we also see God as Creator, Sustainer, Ruler, Father, and Judge. These foundational blocks are essential for framing a Christian worldview.

Paul proclaimed the whole of nature and of history, and he appealed to philosophy and literature, those elements which we believe to be at the heart of a liberal arts curriculum. He emphasized the greatness of God, who is not only the Beginning and Ending of all things but also the One to whom we ultimately will give account. Paul claimed that these things are known by and in God's creation.

Many people today are rejecting the Christian faith not because they perceive it to be false but because they believe it is superficial or trivial. People are looking for an integrated worldview that brings coherence to all learning and helps make sense of life's experiences, some of which are quite confusing.

The comprehensiveness of Paul's message and the insights of his strategy are magnificent, yet the motivation for these things cannot be overlooked. We do not often think as Paul thought, see as he saw, feel as he felt because we do not understand the comprehensive nature of the Christian faith as Paul did. Authentic Christian thinking appreciates the greatness, goodness, and glory of God—pondering His sheer wonder and majesty. Right thinking about God challenges the presuppositions of our contemporary culture, both secular and Christian, which in their current forms seem to be pragmatic, disjointed, and unconnected. Concentrating on the comprehensiveness of the Christian faith compels us to deny these false ideas and instead to begin to see life in a systemic and integrated manner.

When Paul walked around Athens, he did not just notice the idols, but he observed, considered, and reflected on their significance. In our observing, we often look too quickly and read too fast. We need to learn to see and read and then think and reflect from a God-centered perspective. After we have sought to be students of culture, we are then able to appreciate the good, the true, and the beautiful and to confront the false values that are lodged and displayed within culture. Therefore, the challenge of integrating the Christian faith and all learning involves perception, appreciation, engagement, and then, when necessary, confrontation—in that order.

In many ways our post-Christian Western culture in general, and American culture in particular, resembles the pre-Christian Athens of Paul's day, particularly in the focus on the new, the novel, and the world of chance as emphasized by the Epicureans. Our culture is similarly enthralled by novelty. C. S. Lewis, in his famous collection of essays, *God in the Dock*, in which he highlights the value of classic works, maintains that we are obsessed with the new and the novel. Truth and values in our culture of novelty seem to be of little concern or consequence. Paul models for us and thereby invites us to integrate Christian truth in culturally relevant ways and to communicate and live this truth in the midst of an incredibly superficial world.

Superficiality is present when people deal with issues apart from the true reality that ultimately gives them meaning. One can be an expert in one area and fail to connect that area with reality, namely God Himself, resulting in a superficial understanding. Unfortunately most information to which we are exposed on a daily basis falls into this category—whether in literature, media, music, film, many educational enterprises, social interaction, and, God forbid, sometimes even among religious matters.

Thus, our goal at Christian universities in every course must be to engage the subject matter, the true and various options associated with it, and issues of our day in the various areas of learning while recognizing that God, the Source of all truth, is central in every discipline. Harold Heie maintains that such integrated knowledge is a realizable ideal for any academic discipline. The integration of faith and knowledge is the most distinctive task of Christian higher education—always was, is now, always will be. This ideal involves not only the study itself but also the motivation for the study. We can see God behind it all and over it all, whether in math, art, science, literature, or other fields of study.

Unless we understand the impact of this thinking discipline across the campus, then we are not really education with and from a Christian worldview for the glory of God. This does not, as some opponents of faith-learning integration have argued, transform all disciplines into religion studies. Rather, as Charles Wesley penned in his hymn, we are uniting "the pair so long disjointed—knowledge and vital piety."

This uniting of faith and learning then is the essence of Christian higher education. That is the call of the hour and the distinctive approach to education where all teaching and all learning must take place with a view toward reality found only in the glory and grandeur of God. We now turn our attention to the meaning of community in academic contexts that are shaped by this faith and learning dynamic.

Sources

Blamires, Harry. *The Post Christian Mind: Exposing Its Destructive Agenda.* Ann Arbor: Servant, 1999.

Bringle, Robert G., Richard Games and E. A. Malloy. *Colleges and Universities as Citizens.* Boston: Allyn & Bacon, 1999.

Burtchaell, James T. *The Dying of the Light: The Disengagement of Colleges and Universities from Their Christian Churches.* Grand Rapids: Eerdmans, 1998.

Colson, Charles, and Nancy Pearcey. *How Now Shall We Live?* Wheaton: Tyndale, 1999.

Dembski, William A. *The Design Inference.* Cambridge: Cambridge University Press, 1998.

Dockery, David S., and David P. Gushee, eds. *The Future of Christian Higher Education.* Nashville: Broadman and Holman, 1999.

Groothius, Douglas. *Truth Decay*. Downers Grove: InterVarsity, 2000.

Harrison, William H. "Loving the Creation, Loving the Creator: Dorothy L. Sayers's Theology of Work." *Anglican Theological Review*, Spring 2004.

Haynes, Stephen R., ed. *Professing in the Postmodern Academy*. Waco: Baylor University Press, 2002.

Heie, Harold, ed. *The Reality of Christian Learning: Strategies for Faith-Discipline Integration*. Eugene, OR: Wipf & Stock, 2004.

Holmes, Arthur F. *All Truth Is God's Truth*. Grand Rapids: Eerdmans, 1977.

Hughes, Richard T., and William B. Adrian, ed. *Models for Christian Higher Education*. Grand Rapids: Eerdmans, 1997.

Kuklick, Bruce, and D. G. Hart, ed. *Religious Advocacy and American History*. Grand Rapids: Eerdmans, 1997.

Kuyper, Abraham. "The Stone Lectures." Princeton University, 1898.

Lewis, C. S. *God in the Dock: Essays on Theology and Ethics*. Oxford: The Estate of C. S. Lewis, 1970.

Marsden, George. *The Outrageous Idea of Christian Scholarship*. Oxford: Oxford University Press, 1997.

_____. *The Soul of the American University*. Oxford: Oxford University Press, 1994.

McCullough, Donald. *The Trivialization of God: The Dangerous Illusion of a Manageable Deity*. Colorado Springs: NavPress, 1995.

Myers, Kenneth. *All God's Children and Blue Suede Shoes*. Wheaton: Crossway, 1989.

Newman, John Henry. *The Idea of a University*. Notre Dame: University of Notre Dame Press, 1982. First published in 1873.

Noll, Mark. *The Scandal of the Evangelical Mind*. Grand Rapids: Eerdmans, 1995.

Pelikan, Jaroslav. *The Idea of the University: A Reexamination*. New Haven: Yale University Press, 1992.

Piderit, John J. "The University at the Heart of the Church." *First Things*. June/July 1999. 22–25.

Polhill, John. *Acts*. New American Commentary. Nashville: Broadman & Holman, 1992.

Rorty, Richard. *Objectivity, Relativism, and Truth*. New York: Cambridge University Press, 1991.

Sayers, Dorothy. *Creed or Chaos?* Manchester, NH: Sophia Institute Press, 1996.

Schwenn, Mark. "A Christian University: Defining the Difference." *First Things*, May 1999, 25–31.

Sloan, Douglas. *Faith and Knowledge: Mainline Protestantism and American Higher Education*. Louisville: Westminster/John Knox, 1994.

Stott, John R. W. *The Message of Acts: The Spirit, the Church, and the World*. Downers Grove: InterVarsity, 1990.

Wells, David. *Above All Earthly Powers: Christ in a Postmodern World*. Grand Rapids: Eerdmans, 2005.

Williams, Donald. *The Life of the Mind: A Christian Perspective*. Grand Rapids: Baker, 2002.

Wilson, Douglas, and Roy Atwood. *The Quest for Authentic Higher Learning*. Moscow, ID: Canon, 1996.

Note: *This chapter has adopted and adapted key ideas from the significant articles by Mark Schwenn and John J. Piderit.*

6

Envisioning a Shared Community of
Tradition, Belonging, and Renewed Minds

*"That you are standing firm in one spirit,
with one mind, working side by side for
the faith of the gospel."*

Philippians 1:27

*"Real Community is mediated as we are stirred to love of
neighbor through shared love in and through Christ."*

Jean Bethke Elshtain, *Who Are We?*

*"The Christian community is not an ideal we have
to realize, but rather a reality created by God
in Christ in which we may participate."*

Martin Luther, "Gospel for the
Early Christmas Service"

*"In an age of reality, the practice of truth is the only way
to take seriously our protestations concerning truth."*

Francis Schaeffer, *The God Who Is There*

e are called to be Christian scholars and teachers in a world of rapid and incalculable change.
Those who lived through the twentieth century
observed the world progress from horse and buggy to the space
shuttle, literally the transformation of transportation. But the
rate of change has multiplied many times over in recent years.
More information has been generated in the last three decades
alone than in the previous three thousand years. It is reported
that nearly four thousand books are published each day. A
single weekday edition of *The New York Times* includes more
information than the average person in seventeenth-century
England encountered over the course of a lifetime.

Such rapid change has not only impacted our lives but
has great implications for our efforts to build community at
Christian colleges and not just community in general but
Christ-centered communities. To build such communities, we
will need priestly ears and responsive hearts to help us hear,
interpret, and understand our world.

Our society is now characterized by secularism, pluralism,
relativism, and the rise of "new" spiritualities. The word *religion* now conveys ideas of New Age and Eastern mysticism.
The result is a culture grasping for a sense of community
and confused about what direction to take. Moreover, this
culture has lost a sense of shame. University of Chicago professor Jean Bethke Elshtain, in her recent volume *Who Are
We?*, concludes that our society cannot survive without a
sense of shame. When shame is lost, the future of our society
is up for grabs.

It is a chaotic world that Will Willimon describes as one
without meaning, suggesting that the current generation of
teens and twenty-year-olds is an abandoned generation. Our

society has lost a sense of propriety under a misguided understanding of freedom and individualism. Colgate University professor Barry Alan Shain, in his highly esteemed work *The Myth of American Individualism*, argues that freedom depends on a sense of accountability established by community parameters. We need to reclaim this sense of community.

The Lone Ranger concept of the teacher/scholar has developed over the years as the university has passed from premodern to modern and into postmodern times. I believe the Lone Ranger concept has become more prominent as the academy has become more specialized, as concepts of truth and faith have been discredited, and as interdisciplinary and cross-disciplinary work has become less appreciated. All of these things point to the fact that one of the key issues facing Christian universities in the twenty-first century is the challenge to rebuild community on our campuses.

Sociological and Academic Trends

Sociologist Peter Berger has suggested three dominant sociological trends in contemporary culture that have influenced current life and thought in the academy, as well as society at large. These are (1) secularization, (2) pluralization, and (3) privatization. While each of these powerful forces has had a shaping influence, it is privatization that has so influenced our subject for this chapter. Privatization is that process by which modernity has produced a cleavage between the public and private spheres of life, with a focus on the private sphere as the special arena for the expression of individual freedom and fulfillment. This results in a compartmentalized life made up of "many worlds" or "pockets of experience." Life commitments become not matters shared publicly in and among community but merely matters of personal preference or opinion. We are left only with individualism where the individual alone is autonomous in terms of destiny and accountability. In the end we answer to no one but ourselves.

Both the academy and Western culture at large have been moving in this direction for decades. The implications of these shifts for young faculty coming out of secularized Ph.D. programs to Christ-centered universities may be self-evident to some, but the differences are not always so obvious to many of those just completing their programs. These young scholars, prepared in the Berlin research model of doctoral programs, have developed unique specializations. They have often mastered a narrow slice of material in their discipline. Their research has generally taken place with few other colleagues and even at times without the assistance of any other peers.

To borrow the words of Harvard scholar Robert Putnam, we have the ultimate example of "bowling alone." Almost without noticing, Putnam observes, we have been pulled apart from one another and overtaken by a treacherous rip current. We have become lost in our own self-preoccupation. We have learned to succeed in our academic disciplines without colleagueship or relationships.

In addition, research-focused doctoral programs have emphasized developing new ideas or concepts or methods on the one hand while challenging older ones on the other, what we proudly call "original research." We have then, in general, been pushed by our doctoral mentors and advisors to challenge tradition. This original research calls for a kind of analysis and thought that encourages skepticism of others' research and conclusions. Without realizing it, our doctoral work has led us to ignore relationships in our work, to challenge the value of tradition, and in some ways even to discount the importance of trust. Yet Stan Gaede, in his marvelous book *Belonging*, contends that the hallmarks of community are just these very things: *relationships*, *tradition*, and *trust*.

The challenge is further complicated by the nature of specialization. As scholars we are challenged to master one area of knowledge that is sometimes so specialized we often cannot even explain our work to our spouses or our closest friends. The interconnectedness of our work has seemingly become unimportant or has gotten lost along the way.

But it is not just the practices of doctoral research, the rise of specializations, and the cultural shifts toward individualism and privatization that have created the Lone Ranger mind-set among faculty. That combination would certainly be enough of a challenge to address. But we also have to contend with the ever-changing nature of corporate institutional life in these early years of the twenty-first century.

The attempt to create administrative efficiency and order within the context of corporate North America has led to the rise of expanding numbers of staff members and administrators who carry on the work of the college or university so that faculty no longer have to be involved in the life of the institution in quite the same way. Yet we believe the corporate model is insufficient for truly creating a sense of authentic community in our institutions.

The influential sociologist Max Weber, in his work *Economy and Society*, has identified two types of connections that are helpful in thinking about our institutions. The first model, *Gesellschaft*, describes an institution based on contractual links and obligations. In this model major issues are addressed not through relationships but through contracts. Faculty thus relate to an institution not so much out of a sense of belonging but through clearly established contractual arrangements. This means that the administration often functions over against the faculty with authority and responsibilities for the growing bureaucratic complexity of university life that we have come to take for granted and which tends to define our reality at the beginning of the twenty-first century. None of us are so naive as to think that our institutions can exist without contractual links. Aspects of this model are necessary for the world in which we find ourselves.

Yet we would like to suggest that Weber's second model, Gemeinschaft, is a better fit for our Christ-centered institutions. This model describes a community where people have a sense of belonging together and being linked through emotional ties. In such a community people feel they share purposeful work that promotes a common life together. The quest for the experience of community and family and belonging needs to be the overarching vision, so important for contexts like those in which we serve.

We certainly must have institutions aware of and sensitive to the realities of the first model. We must, however, seek to build the second model at each of our campuses. The competing legal and societal demands on our campuses will cause these two models, these two worlds if you will, to function in tension. But we can take steps to address this challenge to community just as we can overcome the ones identified earlier.

There are two more challenges to address before discussing the distinctive nature of what it means to be a Christ-centered community. The first of these challenges grows out of insights from Gaede's previously mentioned work, *Belonging*. This first matter calls for us to recognize that while community was largely built into the structure of institutions of medieval and pre-Enlightenment times, it was largely an ascribed community passed on by tradition. Yet if our institutions are going to have a sense of community, it will be a "created community," not an "ascribed community," and one created by the vision of the institution leadership and by the choice of faculty leaders.

The second matter grows out of Robert Putnam's most insightful and best-selling work, *Bowling Alone: The Collapse and Revival of American Community*. Putnam suggests that there are "bridging communities" and "bonding communities," communities that exist for our private good and others for the public good. Many faculty members who function as Lone Rangers on their campuses nevertheless function in bridging communities within the academic guild.

Thus the first loyalty of some faculty members is not to the institution but to the discipline. They relate to the institution as independent contractors, following the *Gesellschaft* model. The primary relationships of the chemistry professor, for example, are to the American Chemical Society and to the colleagues and research work taking place there. The faculty member experiences "bridging community" but not necessarily "bonding community." The result of this experience of community—from the standpoint of the college or university—is more of a private good for the professor than a public good for the university, though of course it indeed could be both. The vision for the kind of community called for with a *Gemeinschaft* model is a bonding community that certainly brings about private good but also public good for the benefit of all who share in this sense of family and community.

From Lone Ranger to Christian Community

To move from Lone Ranger to Christian scholar/teacher in community, indeed, is a significant challenge. We have to recognize the shifts in culture at large, the rise of individualism and privatization, and the breakdown of interconnectedness from discipline to discipline caused by the rise of specialization and the fragmentation of knowledge. When these concerns about the context in which most all faculty and administrators complete their graduate work—a context which seemingly rejects tradition, ignores relationships, and breaks down trust—are combined with concerns about the very nature of the corporate contexts in which higher education is carried out, we begin to recognize the multiple challenges for envisioning—even choosing to try to create and participate in—bonding communities that exist for the public good of all (*Gemeinschaft* at its best).

The goal of faculty development programs at Christian universities involves, among other things, taking capable and bright scholar/teachers influenced by our culture, by streams of modernity and postmodernity, by the shaping role of the secular research-oriented doctoral programs, by the trends toward individualism and privatization, by growing disciplinary specialization (not to mention the corporate model that so pervasively defines higher educational institutions at-large) and bringing them into new contexts while introducing them to a fresh vision for higher education.

Stan Gaede says that community cannot exist without a shared vision. We must envision and then invite others to join in this vision for a shared purpose—for "life together," to borrow the words of Dietrich Bonhoeffer. This vision helps the scholar/teacher see that the community is larger than self; that its meaning transcends the meaning that one individual may give it; and that its significance comes from God, the One who created it, rather than from those for whom it was created. Thus, we seek to build community within the context of a specific tradition that is rooted in an overarching transcendent vision.

And if that is not swimming upstream enough, here is the most important issue of all: this bonding community in which we want to be involved and invested is a faith-based community, a Christ-centered community, grounded in a commitment to a Christian worldview that can and will be able to engage the culture.

In the early church the longest leap in a Gentile's conversion from polytheism to faith in the Lord Jesus Christ was not renouncing the many for the one but embracing a transformed understanding of ultimate reality. For Gentiles who converted to Christianity, divine power became intimately linked to the values and practice of justice and mercy in interpersonal relationships and social institutions. Thus, in a similar step, an invitation to teach at a Christ-centered institution is an invitation not just to teach, not just to do research, not just to pursue truth, not just to invest in the lives of students, not just to develop relationships with colleagues who are choosing to create a sense of community—as vital as all of these things are—but also to join in building a distinctive Christ-centered community. For to do less would be to fall short of the distinctive calling of Christian scholars and teachers.

Building community, choosing to be a part of community is a most significant step. But more than that, we need to recognize that we must choose to create a sense of community which ultimately exists to bring glory to Jesus Christ and His kingdom.

This means that the highest motive in such a community is the glory of Jesus Christ, a concern for His majesty and glory in all things. Therefore, the Christian college community must be centered in and grounded in Jesus Christ. This means more than merely employing Christians to serve in our institution as important as that is. It is more than having practicing Christians who bring a sense of genuine piety to their task. It means learning together to think and live in accordance with the Christian intellectual tradition and the ideals of the New Testament itself.

Building Blocks for Building a Community with Renewed Minds

Romans 12 is where we turn for guidance for building this community that we envision. Let's look at Paul's portrait in this chapter, which is a picture of a community of renewed minds grounded in the Holy Trinity, for we derive our life, strength, stability, identity, and purpose from God the Father, Jesus the Son, and God the Holy Spirit. The principles expounded in this great chapter provide building blocks to help pull us out of our autonomous individualism and self-centeredness and direct us toward God Himself and toward one another.

What stands out for us is Paul's vision for a Trinitarian, God-centered community. He does not think of it as a human institution but as a divine community. The apostle's vision for this divine community, as an instrument of encouragement and strength for one another, and as an instrument of grace and peace before a watching world, is, I believe, an inviting vision for Christian universities as well.

In Paul's writing (in Rom 12:3–8; 1 Cor 12; Eph 2:11–21; Gal 3:16–29), he celebrates unity in variety: a variety of gifts, a variety of experiences and social classes, and variety in gender and ethnicity. Unity in this variety is possible because of the shared hope for an authentic community. In Romans 12:9–21 the apostle provides a dozen building blocks to help us both address the challenges we have identified and envision a community of tradition, belonging, and renewed minds at Christian universities.

Block 1 (v. 9). We see that Christlike love is the first step toward the kind of authenticity that is needed, a love that is sincere without hypocrisy. Love and hypocrisy exclude each other because love is the epitome of virtue while hypocrisy is the epitome of vice. An authentic love and a loving authenticity should not be confused with perfection. Rather, a loving authenticity will reach out toward others in spite of our frailties and clay feet.

Block 2 (v. 9). This same verse points us to our second building block, which reminds us of the need for discernment. Here we learn that authentic love is not blind sentiment but actually hates what is evil. A loving authenticity is incompatible with anything that opposes the good. While our goal is to build a community of openness and acceptance, we recognize the need for discernment and boundaries in building a community of renewed minds under the lordship of Jesus Christ.

Block 3 (v. 10). An authentic community is also characterized by devotion to one another. Paul brings together two family words to describe this devotion: *Philadelphia*—brotherly or sisterly love—and *philostorgoi*—family affection like a mother's care. Thus we are to relate to one another in an affectionate, self-giving, and devoted way. The powerful combination of these words shows the kind of devotion that brings about unity in the midst of variety, thus uniting our academic communities.

Block 4 (v. 10). The next building block is another important "one another" statement calling for us "to honor one another," showing the mutual affection and honor that is needed among us. We are to seek to outdo one another in showing honor—a kind of competition in doing good.

Block 5 (v. 11). An authentic community is enthusiastic but not in some shallow "rah-rah" sense. Enthusiasm comes from two Greek words: *en theos*, meaning "filled with God." The kind of community we envision is zealous for what is true and fervent in desiring good for one another. This kind of zeal, this kind of enthusiasm recognizes that love of others is in fact a way of serving the Lord; it is a practical outworking of our service to and worship of the Trinitarian God.

These building blocks are essential for creating authentic community. People today are searching for a sense of purpose, significance, security, and belonging. The Christian message addresses all of these matters, but today belonging may be the most important for people in our culture. Creating a sense of belonging can and will deepen our corporate identity; it will enable our student life efforts; it will help attract quality students, as well as excellent staff and faculty members; it will enhance our student retention and thus strengthen the overall academic programs on Christian college campuses.

Block 6 (v. 12). Our next building block calls for patience and faithfulness in our hope. We need a shared hope for our future that frames the way we live, which will enable us to persevere when tough times comes.

Block 7 (v. 13). An authentic community is generous. We need members of this kind of community—trustees, alumni, and friends—who will believe in this work and share generously. Christian colleges and universities will need significant funding and hundreds of generous men and women who will open their checkbooks for the overall good of this work.

Block 8 (v. 13). One of the important marks of conversion in Paul's mission work in Philippi recorded in Acts 16 is hospitality. We must work hard to help all who are part of Christian academic communities to feel welcome. Such a welcoming spirit will greatly enhance a sense of belonging across the campuses. Paul points to two diverse groups in verse 13. We can apply his words by declaring that we will be hospitable to those like us and to those different from us. Moderates will welcome conservatives; African-Americans will welcome Caucasians; those who participate in Greek systems will welcome independents; intramural participants will welcome varsity athletes; nationals will welcome internationals; Republicans will welcome Democrats; and faculty, staff, and administration will all welcome both undergraduate and graduate students. We will seek to serve one another and pursue opportunities to reach out to one another.

Block 9 (v. 14). We will seek to bless others and live at peace with all. We will choose to believe the best about our colleagues until the worst is proven; and if the worst is ever proven, then we will grieve rather than gossip.

It is inevitable in an academic community that friction will develop between people. Bumps and bruises will come. There are times when people will feel slighted or overlooked. People will put others down. Still we are called to live at peace with others in so far as it depends on us. We can't control others, but we can, with God's help, bless them.

Wagging tongues, gossiping, damaging information, and loose lips create strife and division. Instead we need to speak well of others and seek to overcome evil with good.

Negative words work in politics—national politics, local politics, denominational politics, and campus politics—but they are dreadful for creating authentic community. There is no better way to live at peace with others than to express positive wishes, prayers, and good deeds for those who are negative toward us. Similarly we will reach out to other Christian traditions in an irenic way while anchoring our own commitments in the great orthodox intellectual tradition and the *consensus fidei* of the church.

Block 10 (v. 15). Those who make up the kind of community we are envisioning will seek to <u>identify with one another</u> in the different situations of life. We will seek to rejoice with those who rejoice and mourn with those who mourn.

Block 11 (v. 16). Those with renewed minds will <u>seek harmony with others.</u> We live and serve together out of a shared identity, a shared mission, and shared basic convictions. A sense of authentic belonging will in turn create genuine solidarity. Even with the many commonalities shared across a Christian university campus, numerous differences remain: difference in background, experience, ethnicity, perspective, and on and on. Yet in the midst of our many differences, we will endeavor to work together harmoniously. Harmony is not unison. We will sing different parts and play different instruments while nevertheless performing the same symphony with its beautiful harmonies.

Block 12 (v. 16). Our final block is perhaps one of the most important. Academic communities by their nature tend to promote arrogance. We need genuine humility. Snobbery and arrogance can destroy authentic community as quickly as anything.

When we recognize that all that we are, all that we have, all that we have accomplished are gifts from God's divine favor, it will help promote true humility among all of us.

Toward a Faithful Community

Allen Guelzo has recently penned a fine article in *Books and Culture* called "Cracks in the Tower," pointing out some of the shortcomings in Christian higher education. But I believe that an intentional focus on creating a sense of authentic belonging and envisioning a shared community of renewed minds will go a long way in addressing many of the obvious and perceived cracks.

The calling to move from "bowling alone" to strengthening a place of belonging in which scholars, educators, staff, leaders, and learners live, share, serve, and relate together in authentic community is a high and noble calling. It is one not only worthy of envisioning, not only of choosing, but one worthy of our full pursuit and commitment. Grace is needed to build such a sense of community. In that light we turn our attention to the development of grace-filled communities.

Sources

Banks, Robert. *Paul's Idea of Community*. Grand Rapids: Eerdmans, 1980.

Barrett, C. K. *A Commentary on the Epistle to the Romans*. San Francisco: Harper & Row, 1957.

Bellah, Robert, et al. *Habits of the Heart*. San Francisco: Harper & Row, 1985.

Berger, Peter. *The Desecularization of the World*. Grand Rapids: Eerdmans, 1999.

_____. *The Sacred Canopy: Elements of a Sociological Theory of Religion*. Garden City, NY: Anchor/Doubleday, 1969.

Bonhoeffer, Dietrich. *Life Together*. San Francisco: Harper, 1954.

Cranfield, C. E. B. *A Critical and Exegetical Commentary on the Epistle to the Romans*. 2 vols. Edinburgh: T&T Clark, 1975–79.

Elshtain, Jean Bethke. *Who Are We?* Grand Rapids: Eerdmans, 2000.

Gaede, Stan. *Belonging*. Grand Rapids: Zondervan, 1985.

_____. *When Tolerance Is No Virtue*. Downers Grove: InterVarsity, 1994.

Gilbert, James. *Redeeming Culture*. Chicago: University of Chicago Press, 1997.

Guelich, Robert A., ed. *Unity and Diversity in New Testament Theology*. Grand Rapids: Eerdmans, 1978.

Guelzo, Allen. "Cracks in the Tower." *Books and Culture*, July/August 2005.

Guinness, Os. *The Gravedigger File: Papers on the Subversion of the Modern Church*. Downers Grove: InterVarsity, 1983.

_____. *Prophetic Untimeliness*. Grand Rapids: Baker, 2003.

Hardison, O. B., Jr. *Disappearing Through the Skylight*. New York: Viking, 1989.

Johnson, Benton. "Modernity and Pluralism." In *Pushing the Faith: Proselytism and Civility in a Pluralistic World*. Edited by Martin E. Marty and F. E. Greenspahn. New York: Crossroad, 1988.

Longenecker, Richard N. *Community Formation in the Early Church and in the Church Today*. Peabody, MA: Hendrickson, 2002.

McNeal, Reggie. *The Present Future*. San Francisco: Josey-Bass, 2003.

Moo, Douglas J. *The NIV Application Commentary: Romans*. Grand Rapids: Zondervan, 2000.

Oden, Thomas. *After Modernity . . . What?* Grand Rapids: Zondervan, 1990.

_____. *The Rebirth of Orthodoxy*. San Francisco: Harper, 2003.

Postman, Neil. *Technopoly*. New York: Knopf, 1992.

Putnam, Robert. *Better Together: Restoring the American Community*. New York: Simon & Schuster, 2003.

_____. *Bowling Alone: The Collapse and Revival of American Community*. New York: Simon & Schuster, 2000.

Schreiner, Thomas. *Romans*. Baker Exegetical Commentary on the New Testament. Grand Rapids: Baker, 1998.

Sedgwick, Mark. *Against the Modern World*. Oxford: Oxford University Press, 2004.

Shain, Barry Alan. *The Myth of American Individualism*. Princeton: Princeton University Press, 1994.

Stott, John R. W. *Evangelical Truth*. Downers Grove: InterVarsity, 1999.

_____. *Romans*. Downers Grove: InterVarsity, 1994.

Synder, Howard A. *The Community of the King*. Downers Grove: InterVarsity, 1977.

Volf, Mirolslav. "Community Formation as Image of the Triune God." In *Community Formation*. Edited by Richard N. Longenecker. Peabody, MA: Hendrickson, 2002.

Weber, Max. *Economy and Society*. 2 vols. Berkeley: University of California Press, 1978.

White, James E. "Evangelism in a Postmodern World." In *The Challenge of Postmodernism*. Edited by David S. Dockery. Grand Rapids: Baker, 2001.

_____. *Serious Times*. Downers Grove: InterVarsity, 2004.

Willimon, Will, and Thomas Naylor. *The Abandoned Generation: Rethinking Higher Education*. Grand Rapids: Eerdmans, 1995.

Wuthnow, Robert. *Christianity in the Twenty-First Century: Reflections on the Challenges Ahead*. New York: Oxford University Press, 1995.

_____. *The Restructuring of American Religion*. Princeton: Princeton University Press, 1988.

_____. *The Struggle for America's Soul*. Grand Rapids: Eerdmans, 1989.

7

Establishing a Grace-Filled Academic Community

"But grow in the grace and knowledge of our
Lord and Savior Jesus Christ."

2 Peter 3:18

"Fresh spiritual, moral, intellectual and doxological power . . .
is what most of all we long to see."

J. I. Packer and Thomas C. Oden, *One Faith*

"It is in accepting grace that we can begin to model amazing
grace. Only then do we realize how good grace really is."

Charles Swindoll, *The Grace Awakening*

"Grace is the free sovereign favor to the ill-deserving."

B. B. Warfield, *Selected Shorter Writings*

I n previous chapters we have attempted to articulate the importance of rigorous Christian thinking and the distinctives of a Christian worldview. Building on these ideas, we can fashion a vision for a shared common life in an academic community. A Christian university is not a church, yet it is a faith-informed, faith-affirming, and grace-filled community—a distinctive community. Once again we turn to the apostle Paul to find principles to shape our calling as learners, educators, and scholars who seek to carry out our shared purpose with a common spirit.

A Scriptural Guide

In Romans 15:4, Paul writes, "For everything that was written in the past was written to teach us, so that through endurance and the encouragement of the Scriptures we might have hope" (NIV). In Paul's reflection we are reminded that the books of Scripture were primarily intended for those to and for whom they were written in the past. Yet the apostle is persuaded that they were also written to teach us. Scripture is able to make us wise for salvation, which is found only in Christ Jesus. In addition, it also brings us encouragement so that we might have hope, looking beyond time to eternity, beyond present challenges to an eschatological vision and hope. Romans 15:5 suggests that God Himself encourages us through the living voice of Scripture. For God continues to speak through what has been written.

As a Christian academic community, we look first and foremost to Scripture for guidance, but we also recognize that in God's common grace and general revelation we find guidance from history, nature, and experience as we pursue truth in every discipline across the campus. We can affirm this grand reality because we recognize God as the source of all that is true and good and beautiful. Building on this foundation, let us consider several distinguishing marks of community for those of us who live and serve at Christian universities.

Distinctive Marks of a Christian Academic Community

A Call to *Unity*

At the heart of Christian Community is a call to unity. Romans 15:5–6 expresses the hope that the God who gives encouragement (v. 4) will likewise grant a spirit of unity in the community in order that we might engage in the worship and service of God. Thus to live in unity in community is to enjoy the life provided by and in the one true, all-wise God.

What is this unity about which the apostle speaks? It is a unity of spirit and way of thinking that is "according to Christ Jesus." But unity is not the ultimate goal. Unity is simply one stage on the way to the higher purpose of worshipping and serving God.

Our question is this: How is unity possible in such a diverse place as an academic community? We are students, we are faculty; we are staff, we are administrators; we are female, we are male; we are Caucasians, we are people of color; we are from many sections of this country; we are Americans, we are literally from around the world.

While most all who serve or attend a Christian university are Christ-followers, some are seekers. Some have Reformed leanings, and some share more Wesleyan perspectives. We are scientists, we are artists; we are liberal arts proponents, we are professional educators.

We are premodern, we are post-Enlightenment. We are local, we are global. We are Democrats, we are Republicans, and the majority are most likely independents; and the list goes on and on. In the larger academy—of which we are a part, and, we would urge, should contribute an important voice—there exists a veritable Babel of voices clamoring for attention and allegiance in the marketplace where knowledge, beliefs, and opinions are traded. Moreover, in any particular field—whether economics, ethics, political science, history, art, health care, music, philosophy, literature, or the social sciences—there is an absence of a basic consensus regarding either method or conclusions. In the midst of this cacophony, we stand to offer our bid for a coherent picture of life and learning.

Often our opportunities to influence such a context are hampered less by our lack of rigorous thinking or coherent worldview proposals than by the bickering, distrust, and dissensions in the broader Christian community. With the apostle Paul, we would call for Christian academic communities to be agents of reconciliation both in a broken world and for a hurting church, evidencing a unity of mind, spirit, and purpose.

To be sure, there are fights that need to be fought. Paul himself used battle imagery, saying he had "fought the good fight and kept the faith." Fighting the good fight means fighting the right fight, being in the right arena at the right time. Christians are often too focused on the wrong intramural squabbles to have any impact in the society or culture in which we live.

It seems to me that the ultimate danger to the Christian message for the time in which we live lies not in the nuances of our differences but in the rising tides of liberalism, paganism, secularism, and postmodernism that threaten to swamp the Christian message in cultural accommodation.

Yet I am convinced that we can have Christian unity only where the essentials of what it means to be Christian are believed and lived. This does not mean that we cannot and should not have convictions on a wide variety of matters— those which are essential and those that are not. But we need to keep perspective. We need wisdom from Scripture and an informed understanding of history to know which issues are essential to the life of the Christian community and which lie on the periphery.

We are certainly not suggesting that people give up their convictions, nor are we suggesting that we not discuss these various viewpoints with one another. Quite the contrary! We want to encourage these kinds of conversations to take place but with a Christian spirit in the context of a Christian academic community.

With Oxford University's Alister McGrath we would suggest that these conversations and our shared work cannot move forward without confessional boundaries. This, however, does not mean that we should expect or demand uniformity of belief or conviction. Inherent in a historically informed understanding of unity is the need for some flexibility and variety lest we place straitjackets around our community and literally around Scripture itself.

The world in which we live, with its emphasis on diversity and plurality, may well be a creative setting for us to look to what Thomas Oden refers to as a "paleo-orthodoxy for the twenty-first century." Here we can ground our unity not only in the biblical confession that "Jesus is Lord" but in the great tradition flowing from the Apostles' Creed to the confessions of Nicea (325) and Chalcedon (451). The so-called postmodern world could indeed become a rich context for the recovering of a classical view of the Christian tradition. The current scientific emphasis on the interrelationship of all things allows us to speak intelligently of the interdependence of the Christian message historically and globally.

Such historical confessions, though neither infallible nor completely sufficient for all contemporary challenges, can provide guidance when seeking to balance the mandates for right Christian thinking, right Christian believing, and right Christian living. Such historically grounded confessions can also help us think rightly about faith and love in a grace-filled community, pointing out for us the important differences between essentials and nonessentials in Christian doctrine and practice.

As we have noted on other occasions, a useful guide is that those truths on which Scripture and the consensus of the Christian tradition speak with a clear voice are to be considered essentials, whereas whenever biblical Christians equally anxious to interpret and follow Scripture reach different conclusions, these are most likely nonessentials. Of course, this may differ from tradition to tradition, from denomination to denomination. The great confessional tradition, though not the final authoritative word, helps us distinguish primary issues from secondary issues.

An example comes from the affirmation of the Apostles' Creed: We believe in God the Father Almighty, Maker of heaven and earth. To confess God as Almighty has implications for rejecting open theism or process views of God. The affirmation of God as Maker of heaven and earth serves as the beginning confession for a Christian worldview and life view. To affirm God as Creator is the primary tenet of faith. Some can hold to a very old and ancient earth, and others can maintain a young earth created in six twenty-four-hour days. Both viewpoints can be understood to rest within the bounds of the historic Christian tradition.

To deny that God the Father is the Maker of heaven and earth through appeals to naturalism or materialism, however, would clearly fall outside the affirmation not only of Genesis but of the beginning statements of the historical confessions as well. This distinction, of course, does not mean any of these issues cannot be explored. Academic freedom would encourage such exploration. But academic freedom within a Christian academic community means that while all areas except those clearly improper or immoral can be explored, not all things can be advocated or affirmed.

These examples perhaps help us understand that in essentials faith and truth are primary, and we may not appeal to love or grace as an excuse to deny any essential aspects of Christian teaching. In nonessentials then, love is primary, and we may not appeal to personal conviction or zeal as an excuse for failure to exercise grace or demonstrate love. Faith instructs our conscience. Love respects the conscience of others. Faith shapes our liberty; love in a grace-filled context limits its exercise. No one has put it better than Rupert Meldenius (which may have been a pseudonym for Richard Baxter): "In essentials unity. In nonessentials liberty. In all things charity."

Douglas Moo has insightfully noted that God is not necessarily displeased when we hold different views and issues in the Christian community today. When honestly expressed and calmly debated, arguments about various issues can teach us all a great deal. God does not want a bland uniformity in the community of faith, nor is He pleased with believers who do not use their minds to defend their ideas. Dialogue and ongoing conversation about matters over which there is disagreement can help to move the conversation forward and guide us in our common pursuit of truth.

But the key is that all of this takes place under the umbrella of a unified spirit (see John 17). When everyone seeks the good of others and the good of the community as a whole, disagreements can strengthen rather than weaken the community. Ultimately, those who live and serve in a Christian academic community must live in tension, embracing two traits that do not always go together: tenacity in holding to the essentials of the faith and infinite patience and tolerance with people who hold different ideas on the nonessentials.

A Call to *Worship*

Out of a spirit of unity, we praise and serve our great God (Rom 15:6). In Rom 15:5, the apostle Paul asks God to grant the gift of unity to the entire community. As we have seen, this unity is grounded in Jesus Christ Himself. The spirit of unity results in a unity of praise, so that "with one mind and one mouth we glorify . . . God" (v. 6 NKJV). One translation suggests that everyone "can join together with one voice, giving praise and glory to God" (NLT). Here we find our second mark. When this one common aspiration reigns in the Christian community, secondary issues no longer separate hearts and minds. From the internal communion there results common adoration like pure harmony from a concert of well-tuned instruments.

Not only does our unity result in worship, but I believe that our shared worship promotes a common unity. In the ancient church it was affirmed by some that the *lex ordandi* is the *lex credendi*; the law of praying and worship is the law of believing. What this means is that those who can worship our God together through Jesus Christ our Lord can indeed find a common ground for shared service.

The background of Romans 14 and 15 obviously indicates that there was a fragmenting diversity in that ancient faith community—diversity represented between Jew and Gentile, between slave and free, between weak and strong. That diversity was probably not as great as that which surrounds us each and every day on our campuses. But what is important for these Christian college communities is that even with the hierarchal differences that exist within the academic tradition coupled with the cultural and geographical diversity represented on the various campuses, we can come together regularly to offer praise, adoration, and worship to our great and gracious God. In worship the diversity can be enriching, and the hierarchies tend to dissipate at the foot of the cross. Thus we all come to worship as fallen men and women in need of grace.

We believe that worship is a central aspect for defining our shared purpose as a Christian academic community. We believe that the ultimate purpose for believers in every age and every context is the worship and praise of the One who called us unto Himself. To worship God is to ascribe to Him the supreme worth which He alone is worthy to receive. Worship is desired by God and made possible by His grace. To worship God includes reverence and adoration. It also involves a corporate confession of faith as well as Spirit-enabled service expressed in prayer and singing. Worship in the community produces a total way of life that is pleasing to God (Rom 12:1–2). There is thus an obvious and indissoluble relationship between worship and a life of service to God.

Thus a Christian academic community, though not a church, nevertheless must make the worship and praise of Almighty God a high priority. We all assemble in worship in need of God's grace. As we come together, we will seek to provide opportunities where tradition, creativity, and intercultural expression can all be appreciated. We believe that the chapel programs are foundational for a university-wide commitment to integrate faith, learning, and living across the campus. Chapel programs must be carefully designed, clearly communicated, and dynamically led.

A Call to *Service*

Our shared service of learning and teaching involves the whole university as educating agent (Rom 15:14). This third observation recognizes that the Christian university as a whole is an educating agent. Certainly what takes place in the classroom each and every day at the hands of outstanding teaching faculty is primary.

Yet it is myopic to think of the faculty alone as the sole agents of education on a campus. If our educational goals include not only delivering content but also showing the overarching impact of a Christian world and life view and the importance of influencing character development as well, then the out-of-classroom activities on a Christian university campus are more than merely supplemental. Certainly, like any educational institution, Christian universities exist for the sake of instruction that primarily takes place in the class-room or perhaps in some cases in virtual classrooms through technological means.

But it is also important to take notice of what educators sometimes call the hidden curriculum, the activities and services that function on a campus to support classroom instruction. We need to recognize that those who serve in student services, campus ministries, computing services, the library, business and financial services, academic services, facilities, advancement, enrollment, and university relations are also educators or enablers of education. We believe this is a necessary and decisive way to think about a learning community.

Indeed, a Christian college or university in its entirety is a community of learners and educators. Not every educator has the same role. No institution of higher education would exist if instruction and teaching were not at the forefront of what they do, but the formal classroom curricular instruction, though primary, is only the first of numerous ways in which education is accomplished on a campus. This means that all of the practices of the institution as a whole are significant for carrying out its mission.

Yale University philosopher Nicholas Wolterstorff has suggested that education must also involve a focus on tendencies. An emphasis on how we live must be coupled with the primary emphasis on how and what we think. While we recognize that there is some truth to be found in various educational theories, such as a maturationist or student-centered approach to learning, or a socialization or society-centered approach to education, a God-centered model is what Wolterstorff maintains must be at the heart of a Christian institution.

The ultimate goal of Christian higher education then is not simply the maturation of the student, though it is important that maturation takes place. It is not simply the socialization of the student, though that likewise is important. The goal of Christian higher education involves students, staff, and faculty learning and teaching together, keeping faith with God whom we remember and in whom we hope. The learning communities in which we live and serve helps us understand the Christian way of being in the world—a way of responsible, worshipful, and appreciative gratitude. For in this way we learn to see God as the giver of every good and perfect gift and the source of all that is true and beautiful in this world.

Such an understanding of education certainly calls for rigorous academics but also for an unapologetic Christian commitment. This means that all teaching and learning is to be grounded in a Christian worldview and life view. But a Christian worldview and life view which emphasizes the importance of "thinking Christianly" must be extended to involve "living Christianly."

In no way does this holistic vision downplay the long-standing commitment on Christian college campuses to the liberal arts tradition. Nor does it take away from the serious commitment to professional preparation. We should not see this holistic God-centered approach in conflict with helping students become critical thinkers. Learning within the framework of a Christian worldview and life view helps open our eyes to the astonishing pattern of creation when we study science. The study of music moves us to the depths of our being. The understanding of art opens our eyes to appreciate the awesome work of the Creator God. We recognize that art and literature and music are all gifts of God for humanity. This recognition does not necessarily place us over against culture, but it helps us to engage culture from a particular vantage point or perspective. Knowledge must itself reflect a Christian way of being in the world, and thus we learn to see the world from a Christian perspective.

We acknowledge that it is not customary in today's academy to think along these lines. It would be easier for us to follow the accepted path where knowledge is divided and fragmented along disciplinary lines. But fragmentation leads to a situation where facts and values are separated. Facts are assigned to scientists or mathematicians or philosophers without regard to values.

The other path to be avoided is a pietistic form of Christianity that deemphasizes the Christian intellectual tradition. Observing the pietistic emphasis among many Christians has led some to suggest that God would first have to educate people and then convert them before they could have a "Christian mind." Both the fragmented academic model and the pietistic model seem shortsighted. What we need is a holistic vision of learning that not only impacts Christian thinking but also influences Christian living. This vision is especially important for recognizing that what we learn is learned in the context of community and in shared relationships with one another. Thus we live and learn in relationship.

Christian higher education does not educate only to serve some practical end. We should truly delight in the kind of learning which leads to the worship and gratitude of God, the source of all truth. We may also delight in the building up of community. For those engaged in this approach to education, this engagement is itself a component of the Christian way of being in the world, so Christian higher education must be characterized by delight in learning and teaching, which in turn leads to worship and service.

In this approach to education, faculty members not only offer discipline-specific content, but they also provide models, give reasons, and influence tendencies. This holistic approach can help us more fully to become authentic Christian academic communities. It can also extend our efforts to be the community of Christ in the world. As we extend the Christian academic community on campus and become the Christian community in the world, we will be faithful to our calling to engage culture. This engagement helps us to resist the pull toward isolationism. Yet the call to be in the world must likewise strongly resist accommodation.

Successfully steering between isolation and accommodation is one of the great challenges for authentic Christian higher education. It always has been a serious challenge, but today the temptation toward isolation is stronger than in the past, and the lure of accommodation is more powerful than ever. Being "in the world" but not "of the world" reflects the longstanding tension between Jerusalem and Athens. Contrary to Tertullian, we would suggest that Jerusalem does have something to do with Athens. On the other hand, in contrast to Origen and others associated with the School of Alexandria in the third century, we do not think Jerusalem should be cloaked by Athens. Rather, we should recognize the Augustinian tension and seek to live in both Jerusalem and Athens as a Christian academic community representing Christ *to* and *in* the world.

Living in this tension means that we need to recognize that we not only need serious Christian thinking, but we need to encourage modeling of service in the world. If we want to be a grace-filled community, we must model grace. If we want to produce love, we must model love. If we want to emphasize justice, we must model justice.

Such grace, love, and, justice are ready for service and sacrifice, for forgiveness and consideration, for help and sympathy, for lifting up the fallen and restoring the broken. The grace-filled life seeks justice and opportunities for showing mercy. Our understanding of community must somehow include both the celebrative delight in all that is good and the frustrating struggle against injustice. We are to delight in the love we experience and share in advancing the message of love to the world. Thus we delight in all relationships: with God, neighbor, nature, and self, bringing together God's love and justice. Life in community then is an interaction of love.

A Call to *a Shared Life*

The Christian academic community focuses on shared relationships. The final principle that we find in Romans 15 focuses on this interaction in shared relationships—bearing burdens, strengthening weaknesses, and joyfully helping one another. In community we have opportunities to share the burdens of others. Romans 15:2 calls such burden-bearing "neighbor pleasing" or "edifying our neighbors."

The usual antithesis in Scripture is between pleasing God and pleasing humans. Obviously in such a context we please God and never bow to being mere pleasers of men and women. Yet in this context the contrast is between pleasing self and pleasing others. As we live in community with one another, the challenge for us is always to seek the good of others.

Thus on Christian campuses we choose to believe the best about one another. We seek to manifest a spirit of unity. We seek to disagree amicably. When we find ourselves in person-

al conflict, our aim will be to speak in a grown-up ⌐
We will not turn our disagreement into slander. Insi
will seek a God-glorifying resolution. For in Romans ⌐⌐.⌐,
we are told to accept one another just as Christ has accepted
us in order to bring praise to God. In a community with a
common spirit and shared purpose, we will seek to accept
one another. That is what it means to be brothers, to be sis-
ters, to be community.

We recognize that we are all sinners; we are all dependent
on God's amazing and justifying grace. Those who are trusting
in Christ have all been adopted into the same family. We have
all been gifted for service. In such a context it is not enough
to declare that we are all accepted, for we must show acceptance so that we all will experience acceptance.

We can all likely understand and agree with Martin
Luther, who reportedly said that other Christians provide
the best reasons for being a Christian. Simultaneously, he
said, the greatest reasons not to be a Christian are other
Christians. It is because of this realistic assessment of humanity, even redeemed humanity, that we need to promote
an atmosphere of acceptance across the board—faculty accepting staff, staff accepting faculty, faculty and staff working hand in hand with administration who together serve
and invest in the lives of students.

Such an acceptance results in supporting those around us
who are struggling, praying for others when they need it (Rom
15:30), refreshing one another in the way (Rom 15:31–32),
seeing those who are growing weary and offering rest and
words of encouragement. These are qualities of genuine community. If we understand the apostle Paul rightly in Romans
15, it seems that he longed to see these characteristics at the

church of Rome. Likewise, we long to see these qualities in our shared life together on Christian campuses around the world.

A Call to a Grace-Filled Community

John Newton wrote the hymn "Amazing Grace" to tell us of the sweet sound of God's divine favor. When John Bunyan, author of the classic *Pilgrim's Progress*, wrote his own spiritual autobiography, he titled it *Grace Abounding to the Chief of Sinners*. All of us who have experienced grace can also celebrate God's abounding, awakening, and amazing grace.

We experience grace *as pardon*, for it removes our guilt as far as the east is from the west; *as acceptance*, for we are embraced, welcomed, and accepted in God's sight; *as joy and peace*, for it delivers us from the frantic quest for happiness; *as power*, for it transforms us and empowers us; *as hope*, for it gives us confidence in God's plan. There is a close connection between God's gracious activity and God's own character and being. Essentially, to offer praise to His glorious grace is to praise God. Thus we cannot imagine a grace-filled community that is not a God-filled community.

Grace is an overarching term for all of God's gifts to humanity, all the blessings of salvation, all events which are manifested through God's own self-giving. Grace is a divine attribute revealing the heart of the one God, the premise of all spiritual blessing. By grace God freely moves toward us to offer reconciling forgiveness, granting us sonship and daughterhood in the family of God. Grace flows from the Father's goodwill, as it has become mediated to us through the obedient life and sacrificial death of the Son whose mission is completed and mediated to us through the Spirit.

Grace then is the divine favor offered to those who neither inherently deserve nor can ever hope to earn it. It is God's divine disposition to work in our hearts, wills, and actions so as actively to communicate God's self-giving love for humanity.

Grace is not a transaction where God does His part and then we do ours. It is quite the opposite. Grace is a gift. We receive grace not because we are good but because God is good. A salvation so gracious from beginning to end might be misconstrued as encouraging the continuance of sin in the Christian's life, a notion denounced as horrifying by the apostle Paul in most vigorous terms (see Rom 6:2—*mē genoito*, "may it never be!" or "away with such a notion!"). Those who have died to sin cannot go on living in it (Rom 6:2). While works have no part in our salvation, which is solely of grace, good works are to be the centerpiece of the life of gratitude for those who have experienced this divine gift (Eph 2:10; Titus 2:12–14) and thus are to be the centerpiece of such a grace-filled community. Grace is the precious birthright of every believer, and Christian freedom results in an inestimable blessing.

Yet few ideas in Christian history have been more abused than grace and freedom. This freedom is not necessarily economic, social, or political; nor does it refer to freedom in a psychological sense. Certainly emotional health and well-being are desirable goals, but Christian freedom is not an innate quality or state of being which we discover or recover by sorting out past experiences and relationships. Christian freedom is a grace gift to bring release from bondage to sin and freedom for living a life that is blessed.

Christian freedom is not the right to articulate anything we think within the believing community. A community that

is unable to define essential confessional and ethical commitments is not a grace-filled community; in fact, it is a community on the verge of losing its soul. We can err by drawing such boundaries too tight, resulting in an obscurantist
fundamentalism. Equally problematic is the refusal to draw
any boundaries at all, which would result in a thoroughgoing
relativism. We will not go astray if we remember that freedom
is always grounded in grace, and grace is always grounded in
God's ultimate revelation of Himself in Jesus Christ.

What is needed then is not fundamentalist legalism or relativistic libertinism but a living, breathing, healthy, authentic Christian freedom that is present where God's Spirit is
Lord. For as the apostle proclaimed, "The Lord is the Spirit;
and where the Spirit of the Lord is, there is freedom" (2 Cor
3:17). When Paul listed the fruit of the Spirit and the works
of the flesh in Galatians 5:19–23, he presented an outline of
the shape of the grace-filled community, virtues to be extolled
and vices to be shunned. Yet in this passage we do not find the
virtue of freedom. That is because freedom is presupposed in
each one of the virtues: freedom to love, freedom to exude joy,
freedom to manifest peace, freedom to display patience, and
freedom to exercise self-control.

Regrettably, we must acknowledge that Christian presence in the world has moved from idolatrous compromise to
accommodation to adjustment to moral capitulation. When
grace is abandoned, a gradual adaptation of other values en-
sues, ending with the assimilation of Christianity into a de-
spairing postmodernity. Libertines have tended to follow a
graceless accommodation to the spirit of the age. Legalists
seem only to know how to hurl invectives at the idolatries of
this age. Still others seem trapped, unable to listen attentively

to grace. Thus we need not only to hear anew God's word of grace to us, but we need to experience grace anew. Moreover, we need to receive it, model it, show it, and share it. For grace opens us to the things of God and to truth. Grace illumines the intellect, strengthens the will, and guides the senses.

While the idea of grace can be said to be largely a Pauline one (as passed on to us through Paul's children and grand-children: Augustine, Luther, Calvin, and Wesley), there are references to grace in John and Luke as well. John describes Jesus as "full of grace and truth" (John 1:14) and speaks of his followers receiving grace upon grace from the fullness of His grace (John 1:16).

John says that the law, a good thing, came through Moses; but a better thing, grace, came through Jesus (John 1:17). Luke writes that Jesus had grace upon Him (Luke 2:40) and that He increased in favor (or grace) with God and humans (Luke 2:52). In Acts *grace* means not only unmerited favor but also a new power in the Spirit (Acts 1:4,8). Grace is the power with which men and women in academic contexts per-form their gifted task (Eph 4:7; Rom 15:16). Like John, Paul also links grace and truth as related synonyms (cf. Col 1:5–6). But we like the Galatians of old are prone to separate grace from truth, thus becoming grace killers.

How does this happen? By settling for external confor-mity, nullifying God's will by conforming to arbitrary human standards. This can happen in our truth pursuits as well as in other aspects of life. Thus we need an unapologetic confes-sional Christianity to be at the foundation of such a purpose-ful academic community.

Distinctive Commitments of an
Academic Community

Following John Stott, J. I. Packer, Alister McGrath, Thomas Oden, and others, we would suggest that these confessional essentials relate to the three persons of the Trinity—the authority of God in and through Scripture, the majesty of Jesus Christ in and through the cross, and the lordship of the Holy Spirit in and through His manifold life-giving ministries. Thus we should focus on the Trinitarian shape of the Christian faith: (1) in the initiative of the Creator God in *revealing* Himself, (2) in the love of Christ in *redeeming* us from our sins, and (3) in the Holy Spirit in *regenerating* us and facilitating every aspect of thinking and living Christianly.

Therefore, the convictions on which a grace-filled community is built will focus on the Word, the cross, and the Spirit. The convictions needed to shape and form such a grace-filled community unfortunately are often skewed by both libertines and legalists. Let us suggest at least four ways that this can and does take place:

1. Libertines tend to deny the divine nature of Scripture, while legalists tend to ignore the reality that the divine author spoke through human authors while in full possession and use of their faculties, personalities, and vocabularies. Members of a grace-filled community gladly acknowledge the full truthfulness and inspiration of Scripture, affirming its divine-human authorship.

2. Legalists often distrust scholarship and lean toward a thoroughgoing anti-intellectualism, even obscurantism. Members of a grace-filled community, however, acknowledge that all truth is God's truth; that our minds are God-given, being a vital aspect of the divine image we bear; that

we insult God if we refuse to think; and that we honor Him when through science or Scripture we think God's thoughts after Him.

3. Likewise, libertines and legalists both tend to assimilate the world's values uncritically though from opposite ends of the spectrum. A grace-filled community will not conform to the world or withdraw from the world but will seek to transform it and to penetrate it like salt and light.

4. Legalists tend toward separatism, withdrawing fellowship from those who do not agree in every particular point with their own Christian confession. Libertines tend toward a blanket and uncritical ecumenism. The balance between conviction and tolerance, between the explication of truth and the exploration of truth, is not easy to keep; but a grace-filled community must make every effort to do so.

Clearly distinguishing between confessional essentials which cannot be compromised and secondary or tertiary matters (*adiaphora*) is not easy. Some matters beyond those which we have identified as grounded in the Trinitarian God are important in order to maintain denominational distinctives. Yet we must recognize that these denominational distinctives are not necessarily the same as the essential confessional distinctives of orthodox Christianity.

Learning when and how to give deference and freedom in these matters is important for building a grace-filled community; it is the mark of a maturing people. This does not mean that we cannot or should not have biblically informed convictions about such matters. But when godly men and women, after prayer, study, and discussion, disagree on issues like worship practices, church polity, the relationship of church and state, the application of social justice, the use of spiritual gifts by men and women in ministry, the how and when of creation or eschatology, or even the important practices of baptism and the Lord's Supper, we need to give room for freedom of exploration while boldly explicating essential truths. This combination of unity in primary truths and freedom in secondary matters, while preserving love in all situations, should characterize a grace-filled academic community.

The Need for Balance

But a grace-filled community involves more than an orthodox confession, as important and foundational as this is. Participation in a grace-filled community reaches beyond belief to behavior; it brings with it a multifaceted challenge to live accordingly. Legalism in Christian academic communities can be the greatest challenge to grace-shaped freedom.

Regularity in worship, study, or prayer is not to be equated with legalism, nor is spontaneity necessarily a mark of liberty. But a wrong attitude or motive toward either may be legalism. Unrestricted liberty is license. Wrongly restricted liberty is legalism. Rightly restricted liberty for the good of others is love.

Love requires that when persons living in freedom find themselves in a situation where the proper exercise of that freedom would truly offend a brother or sister, then freedom is to be set aside. The basic principle is that personal freedom must be tempered by love for the good of the community.

Finally, grace frees the community to exercise its giftedness in behalf of one another. The fruit of the Spirit identifies the character qualities of love, joy, peace, patience, kindness, goodness, faithfulness, gentleness, and self-control, which are to be emulated. Following the guidelines in Galatians 5, we can identify vices inconsistent with the life of grace, which are to be shunned in this community. Living in a grace-filled academic community means that while we share a common mission, a common vision, a common purpose, and common values, we are not cookie cutters in our actions, in our personalities, in our styles, in our thinking or communication patterns—in the living out of grace on a day-to-day basis.

Grace releases and affirms. It values the dignity of individuals. Grace supports and encourages. Such grace enables us to honor one another through our words and actions while celebrating others' success. Thus a grace-filled community will seek to develop a context in which each person will experience the joy of making significant contributions in the pursuit of excellence, whether in teaching, learning, scholarship, service, the arts, or athletics.

As those who have received grace, we should seek to show and share grace in the workplace, the classroom, the meeting room, the dorm room, the boardroom, and in all aspects of university life. Grace enables us to offer forgiveness when we have been wronged and to claim responsibility and seek forgiveness when we have wronged others. Grace encourages us to shun legalism on the one hand and libertinism on the other in order to work together in harmony and freedom to learn from our mistakes, to differ on academic issues while still maintaining respect for and open communication with one another. Ultimately the grace that has been lavished upon us causes us to recognize our total dependence on God; and thus across our various campuses, we cry out, "Thanks be to God!"

Throughout the previous chapters we have affirmed the importance of essential Christian beliefs as foundational for building intentional communities and systemic Christian universities. We now turn our attention to these important theological foundations.

~~~~~~

Sources

Augustine. *On Christian Doctrine*. Translated by D. W. Robertson. Macmillan Library of Liberal Arts. New York: Macmillan, 1958.

Banks, Robert. *Paul's Idea of Community*. Grand Rapids: Eerdmans, 1980.

Barrett, C. K. *A Commentary on the Epistle to the Romans*. San Francisco: Harper & Row, 1957.

_____. *Freedom and Obligation: A Study of the Epistle to the Galatians*. Philadelphia: Westminster, 1985.

Beker, J. C. *Paul the Apostle: The Triumph of God in Life and Thought*. Philadelphia: Fortress, 1980.

Bloesch, Donald D. *God the Almighty*. Downers Grove: InterVarsity, 1996.

Blunck, J. "Freedom." In *New International Dictionary of New Testament Theology*. Edited by Colin Brown. Grand Rapids: Zondervan, 1978.

Bock, Darrell L. *Purpose-Directed Theology: Getting Our Priorities Right in Evangelical Controversies*. Downers Grove: InterVarsity, 2002.

Bonhoeffer, Dietrich. *The Cost of Discipleship*. Translated by R. H. Fuller. New York: Macmillan, 1959.

_____. *Life Together*. San Francisco: Harper, 1954.

Bruce, F. F. *The Epistle to the Galatians*. New International Greek Testament Commentary. Grand Rapids: Eerdmans, 1987.

_____. *Paul: Apostle of the Heart Set Free*. Grand Rapids: Eerdmans, 1977.

Calvin, John. *Institutes of the Christian Religion.* Translated by Ford Lewis Battles. Library of Christian Classics. 2 vols. Philadelphia: Westminster, 1960.

Corley, Bruce, and Curtis Vaughan. *Romans.* A Study Guide Commentary. Grand Rapids: Zondervan, 1976.

Cousar, Charles B. *Galatians.* Interpretation. Atlanta: John Knox, 1982.

Cranfield, C. E. B. *A Critical and Exegetical Commentary on the Epistle to the Romans.* International Critical Commentary. 2 vols. Edinburgh: T&T Clark, 1975–79.

Diekeme, Anthony J. *Academic Freedom and Christian Scholarship.* Grand Rapids: Eerdmans, 2000.

Dockery, David S. *Biblical Interpretation Then and Now: Contemporary Hermeneutics in the Light of the Early Church.* Grand Rapids: Baker, 1992.

_____, ed. *The Challenge of Postmodernism.* Grand Rapids: Baker, 2001.

_____. "Fruit of the Spirit." In *Dictionary of Paul and His Letters.* Edited by G. F. Hawthorne, Ralph P. Martin, and Daniel G. Reid. Downers Grove: InterVarsity, 1993.

_____. "An Outline of Paul's View of the Spiritual Life: Foundation for an Evangelical Spirituality." *Criswell Theological Review* 3:2 (1989): 327–40.

Dunn, James D. G. *The Theology of Paul the Apostle.* Grand Rapids: Eerdmans, 1998.

Epp, Eldon J. "Paul's Diverse Imageries of the Human Situation and His Unifying Theme of Freedom." In *Unity and Diversity in New Testament Theology.* Edited by Robert A. Guelich. Grand Rapids: Eerdmans, 1978, 100–16.

Fung, Ronald Y. K. *The Epistle to the Galatians.* New International Commentary. Grand Rapids: Eerdmans, 1988.

Furnish, Victor P. *Theology and Ethics in Paul*. Nashville: Abingdon, 1968.

George, Timothy. *Amazing Grace*. Nashville: LifeWay, 2000.

_____. *Galatians*. New American Commentary. Nashville: Broadman & Holman, 1994.

Gilcrest, K. G. "Escaping Fundagelicalism." *Mars Hill Review* 20 (2002): 137–40.

Guthrie, Donald. *Galatians*. New Century Bible. London: Nelson, 1969.

Hart, Jeffrey. *Smiling through the Cultural Catastrophe: Toward the Revival of Higher Education*. New Haven: Yale University Press, 2001.

Hart, Trevor. *Faith Thinking*. Downers Grove: InterVarsity, 1985.

Hawthorne, Gerald. *Philippians*. WBC. Word: Waco, 1983.

Henry, Carl F. H. *The Uneasy Conscience of Modern Fundamentalism*. Grand Rapids: Eerdmans, 1947.

Holmes, Arthur. *Fact, Value, and God*. Grand Rapids: Eerdmans, 1997.

Holmes, Robert Leslie. *The Creed: Life Principles for Today*. Greenville, SC: Ambassador, 2002.

Kelly, J. N. D. *Early Christian Creeds*. New York: Harper, 1976.

Kimmel, Alvin F., Jr., ed. *Speaking the Christian God: The Holy Trinity and the Challenge of Feminism*. Grand Rapids: Eerdmans, 1992.

Ladd, George E. *A Theology of the New Testament*. Grand Rapids: Eerdmans, 1974.

Lightfoot, J. B. *The Epistle to the Galatians*. New York: Macmillan, 1868.

Longenecker, Richard N. *Galatians*. Word Biblical Commentary. Dallas: Word, 1990.

_____. *Paul, Apostle of Liberty*. New York: Harper & Row, 1964.

Lovelace, Richard. *Dynamics of Spiritual Life*. Downers Grove: InterVarsity, 1979.

Luther, Martin. *A Commentary on St. Paul's Epistle to the Galatians* [1535]. Cambridge: Clarke, 1953.

_____. "The Freedom of a Christian [1520]." In *Luther's Works*. Edited by J. H. Grimm. Philadelphia: Muhlenberg, 1957, 31:327–77.

McGrath, Alister. *Evangelicalism and the Future of Christianity*. Downers Grove: InterVarsity, 1995.

_____. *I Believe: Exploring the Apostles' Creed*. Downers Grove: InterVarsity, 1997.

_____. *A Passion for Truth: The Intellectual Coherence of Evangelicalism*. Downers Grove: InterVarsity, 1996.

Mikolaski, Samuel J. *The Grace of God*. Grand Rapids: Eerdmans, 1966.

Moo, Douglas J. *Romans*. The NIV Application Commentary. Grand Rapids: Zondervan, 2000.

Morris, Leon. *Galatians: Paul's Charter of Freedom*. Downers Grove: InterVarsity, 1996.

Mouw, Richard J. *He Shines in All That's Fair: Culture and Common Grace*. Grand Rapids: Eerdmans, 2001.

Oden, Thomas. *After Modernity . . . What?* Grand Rapids: Zondervan, 1990.

_____. *The Rebirth of Orthodoxy*. San Francisco: Harper & Row, 2003.

_____. *The Transforming Power of Grace*. Nashville: Abingdon, 1993.

Packer, J. I., and Thomas C. Oden. *One Faith: The Evangelical Consensus*. Downers Grove: InterVarsity, 2004.

Padgett, Alan G. *Science and the Study of God*. Grand Rapids: Eerdmans, 2002.

Pinnock, Clark H., ed. *Grace Unlimited*. Minneapolis: Bethany, 1975.

Polhill, John B. *Paul and His Letters*. Nashville: Broadman & Holman, 1999.

Ryrie, Charles C. *The Grace of God*. Chicago: Moody, 1963.

Schreiner, Thomas. *Romans*. Baker Exegetical Commentary on the New Testament. Grand Rapids: Baker, 1998.

Snyder, Howard A. *The Community of the King*. Downers Grove: InterVarsity, 1977.

Stott, John R. W. *Evangelical Truth*. Downers Grove: InterVarsity, 1999.

_____. *Romans: God's Good News for the World*. Downers Grove: InterVarsity, 1994.

Swindoll, Charles. *The Grace Awakening*. Dallas: Word, 1990.

Tanner, Kenneth, and Christopher A. Hall, eds. *Ancient and Postmodern Christianity: Paleo-Orthodoxy in the 21st Century*. Downers Grove: InterVarsity, 2002.

Tertullian. *On Prescription against Heretics*. West Orange, NJ: New Advent, reprint 2004.

Webber, Robert E. *Ancient-Future Faith. Rethinking Evangelicalism for a Postmodern World*. Grand Rapids: Baker, 1999.

Wesley, John. *Wesley's Standard Sermons*. Edited by Edward H. Sugden. 2 vols. London: Epworth, 1955–56.

Wolterstorff, Nicholas P. "Christian Higher Education in Reformed Perspective." *Lutheran Education* 134 (1999): 129–40.

_____. *Educating for Responsible Action*. Grand Rapids: Eerdmans, 1980.

_____. *The Project of a Christian University in a Post-Modern Society*. Amsterdam: VU Boekhandel, 1988.

8

Developing a Theology for Christian Higher Education

*"You heard Him and were taught by Him,
because the truth is in Jesus."*

Ephesians 4:21

*"Christian Theology is indeed necessary for the well being
of Christians and of contemporary Christianity."*

James Leo Garrett Jr., *Systematic Theology*

*"Evangelical theology aims not only to be faithful
to Scripture, but also to explore the unfaithfulness
of the Christian community to Scripture."*

Donald G. Bloesch, *Essentials
of Evangelical Theology*

*"Christian theology seeks to understand the God revealed
in the Bible and to provide a Christian understanding
of God's creation, particularly human beings and
their condition, and God's redemptive work."*

Millard J. Erickson, *Christian Theology*

The term *theology* scares many people. It sounds formidable, esoteric, abstract, and technical. Many people are suspicious of the word *theology*—thinking it is irrelevant to our life with God or, even worse, a sort of human presumption. The suspicion of theology is present among many people, not just academics but pastors and numerous laypeople alike. The suspicions are often right, at least in part, because theology often has been studied in the wrong way, which has led to unhelpful or even hurtful thinking at many places.

Theology is not just an attempt to articulate our feelings about our dependence on God, contrary to the nineteenth-century German theologian, Friederich Schleiermacher. On the other hand, it is more than an attempt to state the objective truth, to put the truth in proper order as the great Presbyterian theologian, Charles Hodge, suggested when he attempted to articulate theology in nineteenth-century scientific terms. It seems best to think of theology in a twofold way: (1) as *developing a mind for truth* so that we can indeed articulate "the faith once for all delivered to the saints," and (2) as *developing a heart for God* so that our lives are built up in the faith. Ultimately, a distinctive theology for Christian higher education will have Christ at its center, the church as its focus, and the influencing of culture as a key element of its vision.

Theology can render service to Christian higher education in many ways. It satisfies the mind so that we can know God, so that we can know the living Christ. Theology is vitally important for both the teaching and culture-engaging task (1 Pet 3:15). Theology is necessary as a touchstone for understanding what we believe and for recognizing the principles by which our lives are to be shaped. Such beliefs and practices come from serious theological reflection.

Christian theology therefore also points to ethics. Certainly it is possible to act one way and to think another, but it is not logically possible for us to do so for long, for even the biblical writer has admonished us, "As [a person] thinks in his heart, so is he" (Prov 23:7 NKJV). Since one of the goals of Christian higher education is to help students live in the world with a lifestyle that issues in glory to God, then we must think—and think deeply—not only of personal ethics but of the implications of the biblical faith for social, economic, and political ethics as well. Such necessities touch the heart of the life and mission of Christian higher education.

The Great Tradition of Orthodoxy

Our first steps involve the need to cultivate a holistic orthodoxy, based on a high view of Scripture and congruent with the Trinitarian and Christological consensus of the early church. We would suggest that the shared work of Christian higher education cannot move forward without confessional convictions or confessional boundaries.

We must ground our unity not only in the biblical confession that Jesus is Lord but also in the great tradition flowing from the Apostles' Creed to the confessions of Nicea in AD 325 and Chalcedon in AD 451. Likewise, we must claim the best of the Christian confessional heritage as well. Such historic confessions, though neither infallible nor completely sufficient for all contemporary challenges, can provide guidance in seeking to balance the mandates for right Christian thinking, right Christian believing, and right Christian living.

Such historically grounded confessions can also help us think rightly about faith and about how we relate to one another in love, pointing out for us the important differences between primary, secondary, and tertiary issues in Christian theology and practice. For example, a bedrock primary doctrine essential for us to confess is that salvation is by grace alone, but the different Calvinistic or Arminian expressions of that truth are secondary, not primary. Confessing that Christ will return is a primary doctrine, but defining the nature of the millennium is a secondary or probably even a tertiary matter. The great confessional tradition, though not the final authoritative word, can serve as a tremendously helpful resource for us in distinguishing primary issues from second- and third-order doctrines.

As we take the next step in thinking about a theology of Christian higher education, it is important not only to affirm these central consensus beliefs of the Christian faith, but we must also exclude errors on the right and the left. Errors on the right, such as a dictation view of Scripture or fundamentalist separatism or legalism, must be recognized as faulty thinking in the same way that Paul called out the Judaizers in the book of Galatians. On the other hand, views of so-called Christian existentialism, liberation, or process thought, as well as other thinking less faithful to Scripture, must also be excluded. In our day we must reclaim such bedrock convictions in the midst of a growing secularized academy. This will call for us to swim upstream, but for Christian colleges and universities to be faithful to the Christian character of their institutions, they can do no other.

Thinking Theologically

Some at this time might be asking, "Does this mean that all involved in Christian higher education are to be theologians in the sense of being uniquely summoned to the task of leading in theological thought?" Certainly we would like to encourage all faculty and staff at Christ-centered institutions to be theologians but not theologians in the technical sense of that term. What is needed today is for administrators, trustees, faculty, and staff once again to think lofty thoughts about God and to live accordingly, that is, to live according to God's Word and Holy Scripture. Some theologians suggest that theology essentially is thinking about God. If they are right, and we believe they basically are, then to abdicate the theological domain to specialists alone either because of a lack of interest or because of the technicalities involved is not only harmful to the work of Christian higher education, but we believe also that it is unpleasing to God. The truth is that every believer in the world of Christian higher education is in some sense a theologian, for all believers who know God have the responsibility to see and understand the revelation of God for their foundational beliefs while integrating these beliefs into their calling as academics.

Theology is certainly not the whole of academic life; but there must be a place for the true intellectual love of God; for Jesus has told us to love God with our heart, soul, strength, and mind, and to love our neighbor as well. This should not lead to some cold intellectual approach to the faith unaccompanied by affection. For too many, theology is a kind of intellectual aloofness or uncommitted intellectual curiosity. But before we can develop a theology for Christian higher education, it will be helpful to think about the relationship of theology to both church and culture and also to understand the responsibility of higher education in preparing future church and denominational leaders.

We need to understand history in order to understand better what is distinctive about our denominational traditions. We also need fresh thinking about the relationship of Christian higher education to the church, for it is central to God's working in history. The church is not only central to history but to the gospel and Christian living as well. Thus, theology is more than God's words for me as an individual; theology is God's words for us, the community of faith. It is vitally important that we understand theology not merely in individualistic terms. We need to move to a corporate and community understanding of these ideas. For these reasons the early years of Christian higher education placed their focus first in terms of service for the churches and then more broadly for society.

We have observed that the contemporary discipline-specific separation or fragmentation of knowledge in which we find ourselves in today's academy has resulted in a twofold problem: (1) an unhealthy individuality and (2) a suspicion and hostility of the theological enterprise. Certainly the academy at large, and sometimes even the faith-based academy, does not encourage, and in fact at times seemingly discourages, the need for creative and collaborative efforts of theologians. Unfortunately, there is seldom sufficient cross-fertilization between theologians and the other disciplines within the academy. These groups read different books, listen to different experts, identify different problems, consider different issues, contribute to different journals, and congregate in different groupings as they pursue diverse and sometimes competing agendas.

Our concern is not to be another cantankerous voice on the contemporary scene. Too many people today are looking at these issues and seeing the glass less than half empty. What is needed is a renewed eschatological vision for the people of God with a recognition of the important place that Christian higher education can have in God's overall plan and a fresh appreciation for the significance of a theological foundation for this work. Granted, the lack of theological acumen on the part of many in the academy is due to many factors beyond the control of professional theologians; nevertheless, it is important that we recognize the relationship between faithful theologians and other faithful Christ-centered academics.

Although academic theology has produced vast amounts of materials requiring technical specialization, as is the case in other areas of knowledge, theology, if it is to serve the various disciplines across the academy, cannot afford to become some sort of esoteric endeavor done only for the initiated few. It is germane and important to have theological societies in serious theological debate, but unless Christian theology operates consciously as the servant of both the church and the academy, little long-term value is forthcoming.

The responsibility of making theology helpful to the academy rests both with professional theologians and with other thinkers across the disciplines as well. Theology must be understandable to nonprofessional theologians. Too often what theologians write is unintelligible for many outside the discipline. Lest anyone misunderstand, we think serious theological research and investigation must continue, but that cannot be the end of the theological enterprise.

In the past, theologians of the church wrote so that literate people could understand, and it must be acknowledged that

Augustine, Aquinas, Luther, Calvin, and Wesley are often much easier to read and understand than many contemporary theologians. Today we need theologians who can write in ways that are sharp, powerful, and effective. In this vein the Reformers frequently commended the biblical writers for their clarity, simplicity, and brevity and sought to emulate them in their own writings. If theology is to impact the church and inform others in the world of Christian higher education, theologians must learn to communicate in understandable ways.

Likewise, theology in the academy must be relevant and applicable to other disciplines. Yale theologian Miroslav Volf, in his *Practicing Theology: Beliefs and Practices in the Christian Life,* has encouraged us to think of theology as "a way" in the manner the early church thought of the Christian life as the way of life. This is not in any sense to downplay or belittle the importance of serious Christian scholarship. We recognize that the various disciplines of theology are indeed indispensable to an accurate understanding of truth. Without the scholarship of experts in philosophy, archaeology, history, languages, hermeneutics, and other related fields, theological study itself would be seriously impoverished.

Yet, when these specializations are pursued as an end in themselves and not molded into a unified view of truth, they sometimes get lost in the cacophonous voices across the academy. This certainly should not be heard as subverting the validity and importance of scholarly disciplines. Quite the contrary! But such scholarship neither touches the higher function of theology nor informs the work of Christ-centered higher education unless it sets forth a perspective that depends on the regenerated mind and exposes the radical difference between Christianity and the competing philosophies within the broader academy.

We must admit that some theologians unduly complicate the Christian faith or distract us from aspects of helpful Christian thinking and living. Similarly theology can enable all aspects of Christian higher education to recover a true understanding of human life. In this sense faculty, staff, and students can once again gain a greatness of soul. Theology can help us recover the awareness that God is more important than we are, that the future life is more important than this one, and that a right view of God gives genuine significance to our calling as academics.

Theology can help those called to serve in Christian higher education to better understand what we believe and why we believe it. We can appreciate our heritage and enliven our future hope. When this takes place, Christian colleges and universities can and will be strengthened. The gospel in its fullness can be proclaimed. Without the foundation of solid theology there can be no effective long-term educational efforts that are truly and distinctively Christian.

Our fundamental assumption in this task is that truth is available to us and is found in God's revelation of Himself in creation, history, experience, and ultimately in Christ as made known to us in Holy Scriptures. While we unhesitatingly affirm these truths, a warning needs to be voiced. No single group, church, or denomination, however orthodox, strictly and faithfully follows this revelation from God. While the church has characteristically sought to be faithful to Scripture, the depth of meaning in the biblical text is rarely fully understood at any one moment in history. Theology in any tradition is often the art of establishing central and classic texts, which may mean that the other texts unfortunately are ignored or not given significant weight. No single theologian, church, or denomination has escaped or can escape this frailty though there is certainly continuity throughout the centuries, particularly in the teachings concerning the person and work of the Lord Jesus Christ, which provides the ultimate foundation for our work in Christian higher education.

Theology and the Christian Intellectual Tradition

Thus, understanding theology in the context of the great Christian intellectual tradition of the church at large and within the stream of various denominational traditions can provide insight for today and guidance for the future. In this way theology can help us engage the wrongheaded thinking often evident in today's academy. Knowledge of the past keeps us from confusing what is merely a contemporary expression from that which is enduringly relevant. Theology helps present to the church and the academy a valuable accumulation of enduring insights along with numerous lessons and warnings, both positive and negative. Theology done with the focus on the church and done for the good of the academy will always have one eye on the historical past of the Christian tradition.

Such awareness of the church's history provides a bulwark against the pride and arrogance that would suggest that "we" are the only group or tradition that carries on the orthodoxy of the apostles. Knowledge of such continuities and discontinuities in the past will help us focus on those areas of truth that are timeless and enduring while encouraging authenticity and humility as well as a dependency on God's

Spirit. Hopefully this awareness will cause us not just to accept things in accordance with our tradition or do things in accordance with our own "comfort zones" but will again and again drive us back to the source of our theology in the New Testament with fresh eyes and receptive hearts, thus helping us both to understand the distinctives of Christian higher education and to relate constructively to those outside the Christian tradition.

Some might be asking, "Do these theological commitments stifle honest intellectual exploration?" We do not think so. Our challenge is to preserve faithfully and pass on the Christian tradition while encouraging honest intellectual inquiry. We believe these two things can coexist, even if in tension, in an enriching dialectical dependence.

Guidance and balance in these matters will come as we are faithful in integrating an informed theological foundation with all areas of learning. For Christian academics to address these matters, we must hear afresh the words of Jesus, echoing the emphasis of our opening chapter, from what is called the Great Commandment (Matt 22:36–40). Here we are told to love God not only with our hearts and souls but also with our minds. Jesus' words refer to a wholehearted devotion to God with every aspect of our being from whatever angle we choose to consider it—emotionally, volitionally, or cognitively.

This kind of love for God results in taking every thought captive to make it obedient to Christ (2 Cor 10:5), a wholehearted devotion to distinctively Christian thinking. This means being able to see life from a Christian vantage point; it means thinking theologically across the curriculum.

Beginning Steps

A theologically informed approach to Christian higher education must offer a way to live that is consistent with reality by offering a comprehensive understanding of all areas of life and thought, every aspect of creation. The starting point begins with God and brings us into His presence without delay. The central affirmation of Scripture is not only that there is a God but that God has acted and spoken in history. God is Lord and King over this world, ruling all things for His own glory, displaying His perfections in all that He does in order that humans and angels may worship and adore Him. Such thinking provides a coherent way of seeing life, of seeing the world distinct from deism, naturalism, materialism, existentialism, polytheism, pantheism, mysticism, or deconstructionist postmodernism. Such a theistic perspective provides bearings and direction when confronted with secularistic and pluralistic approaches to truth and morality. Fear about the future, suffering, disease, and poverty are informed by Christian thinking grounded in the redemptive work of Christ and the grandeur of God.

What is needed among those of us who serve in Christian higher education in the twenty-first century is a renewed commitment to Holy Scripture and to our confessional heritage. But not only this, we need (as emphasized in the previous two chapters) to renew our commitment to relate to one another in love and humility, bringing about true fellowship and community, resulting not only in a rebirth of orthodox foundations but also a rebirth of Christian orthopraxy before a watching world.

If Christ-followers lived in the kind of love and unity which the Lord Jesus Christ called for, it would do wonders for converting sinners and enlarging the church of Jesus Christ.

So the choice is not between truth or piety, orthodoxy or orthopraxy. In that sense we need to think of the call for a theology of Christian higher education, not just as an attempt to articulate our feelings about our dependence on God, as the pietists might say, or to describe the great truths of the faith in proper order, as the rationalists might say. Rather, as we said at the beginning of this chapter, it is an attempt to *develop a mind for truth* so that we can articulate the faith once for all delivered to the saints and to *develop a heart for God* so that our lives are built up in the faith.

Some could well be thinking that such commitments as described in this chapter are potentially divisive and thus should be deemphasized in their importance. But these theological commitments are the very backbone, the underpinnings, of distinctive and systemic Christian higher education. Without healthy theology, all of us, whether those of us in the church or the academy, are prone to be tossed back and forth by waves, blown here and there by every wind of teaching (as Paul describes in Eph 4:14). A healthy understanding of theology for Christian higher education will help mature the head and heart, enabling believers to move toward spiritual health, resulting in the praise and exaltation of God.

Those who teach and study in Christ-centered institutions must take to heart the words of the apostle Paul: "Do not be conformed to this age, but be transformed by the renewing of your mind" (Rom 12:2). What we are calling for is certainly intellectually challenging. It is not the easiest road for us to travel, but it is the one faithful to the best of our heritage, and it provides no room for mere anti-intellectual piety, much less some vague spirituality, in Christian higher education. We are to have the mind of Christ; this certainly requires us to think and wrestle with the challenging ideas of history in the issues of our day. For to do otherwise will result in a generation of God's people ill-equipped for faithful thinking and service in this new century. Christian thinking is needed to confront the world. Instead of allowing our thoughts to be captive to culture, we must take every thought captive to Jesus Christ.

Implications

In summary, we would suggest that a theology for Christian higher education can help us develop connecting and unifying principles for Christian thinking, grounded in the truth that God is Creator and Redeemer. A call for a theology for Christian higher education will encourage curious exploration and serious wrestling with the foundational questions of human existence. We believe such a commitment to a theology for Christian higher education will help us develop a comprehensive and historically informed view of what it means to be a part of the great Christian intellectual tradition as we shape the Christian educational enterprise for this new century.

A theology of Christian higher education will help us to be aware of contemporary cultural, social, and religious trends. What we are suggesting will require us to live in tension, reflecting a theological outlook while simultaneously having particular discipline-specific emphases across the curriculum. Sometimes the issues with which we wrestle are filled with ambiguities.

We would be naive not to recognize the times in which we live and the context and culture for which our students are preparing to serve. A theology of Christian higher education rooted in Scripture and grounded in the best of our denominational traditions can equip the work of Christian higher education for times of duress and trial, whether the result of persecution, faithless scholarship, or the church's internal bickering and divisions. What is needed is a bedrock, nonnegotiable commitment to a belief in a triune God—in one mediator between God and humanity, the man Christ Jesus, who was God incarnate.

This commitment represents a belief in a totally truthful and authoritative Bible and in the message of God's justifying work by grace through faith revealed therein. It is rooted in a focus on the church, and it lives in hope of the return of Christ, resulting in a commitment to a life of prayer, holiness, obedience, and growth in Christ.

This kind of theology can shape Christian higher education for a promising future. These truths are not culturally confined, nor are they easily expunged without great peril. What is needed for this time is an ancient kind of orthodoxy, a primitive but passionate core of theological truths that nurtured persecuted believers in the past and will be the only thing to comfort once the flames of suffering are stoked again. If persecution looms on the horizon, then our orthodox commitments must also return—commitments that are firm but loving, clear but gracious, ready to respond to issues and challenges that the culture and world present to Christ-followers but not necessarily responding to every contextual skirmish or intramural squabble.

May God renew Christian higher education as we seek to develop a theology for Christian higher education even as we pray for all involved in this important enterprise. May these commitments not be easily lost or forgotten, but may they remain firmly rooted in our minds and hearts for years and decades to come for the glory of God.

Sources

Abraham, William J. *The Coming Great Revival: Recovering the Full Evangelical Tradition.* San Francisco: Harper & Row, 1984.

Akin, Daniel, ed. *A Theology for the Church.* Nashville: B&H, 2007.

Barr, James. *Beyond Fundamentalism.* Philadelphia: Westminster, 1984.

Bloesch, Donald G. *Essentials of Evangelical Theology.* 2 vols. San Francisco: Harper & Row, 1978–79.

Dockery, David S., ed. *New Dimensions in Evangelical Thought.* Downers Grove: InterVarsity, 1998.

Eliot, T. S. *Christianity and Culture.* New York: Harcourt, Brace, 1940.

Elshtain, Jean Bethke. *Who Are We?* Grand Rapids: Eerdmans, 2000.

Erickson, Millard J. *Christian Theology.* 3 vols. Grand Rapids: Baker, 1983–86.

Fackre, Gabriel. *The Christian Story.* Grand Rapids: Eerdmans, 1987.

Garrett, James Leo, Jr. *Systematic Theology.* 2 vols. Grand Rapids: Eerdmans, 1995.

George, Timothy, and David S. Dockery, eds. *Theologians of the Baptist Tradition.* Nashville: Broadman & Holman, 2001.

Grenz, Stanley J. *Theology for the Community of God.* Nashville: Broadman & Holman, 1994.

Hannah, John. *Our Legacy.* Colorado Springs: NavPress, 2001.

Henry, Carl F. H. *God, Revelation, and Authority.* 6 vols. Waco: Word, 1976–83.

Hodge, Charles. *Systematic Theology.* Grand Rapids: Eerdmans, 1975. First published by Scribner in 1872.

Horton, Michael, ed. *A Confessing Theology for Postmodern Times.* Wheaton: Crossway, 2000.

McGrath, Alister. *Christian Theology*. Oxford: Blackwell, 1994.

Mullins, E. Y. *The Christian Religion in Its Doctrinal Expression*. Philadelphia: Judson, 1917.

Oden, Thomas C. *The Rebirth of Orthodoxy*. San Francisco: Harper and Row, 2003.

Olson, Roger. *The Story of Christian Theology*. Downers Grove: InterVarsity, 1999.

Packer, J. I., and Thomas C. Oden. *One Faith*. Downers Grove: InterVarsity, 2004.

Poe, Harry L. *Christianity in the Academy*. Grand Rapids: Baker, 2004.

Pelikan, Jaroslav. *The Christian Tradition*. 5 vols. Chicago: University of Chicago Press, 1971–89.

_____. *The Vindication of Tradition*. New Haven: Yale University Press, 1986.

Saucy, Robert L. "Doing Theology for the Church." In *The Necessity of Systematic Theology*. Edited by John Jefferson Davis. Grand Rapids: Baker, 1978.

Schleiermacher, Friederich. *On Religion: Speeches to Its Cultured Despisers*. Translated by John Oman. New York: Harper & Row, 1965. First published in German in 1799.

Schmeltekopf, Donald D., and Dianna Vitanza. *The Future of Baptist Higher Education*. Waco: Baylor University Press, 2006.

Volf, Miroslav. *After Our Likeness*. Grand Rapids: Eerdmans, 1988.

_____, ed. *Practicing Theology: Beliefs and Practices in the Christian Life*. Grand Rapids: Eerdmans, 2002.

Wells, David F. *No Place for Truth; or, Whatever Happened to Evangelical Theology?* Grand Rapids: Eerdmans, 1993.

9

Thinking Globally about the Future

"So that we can be co-workers with the truth."

3 John 8

"We think we are headed to the future.
The truth is the future is headed toward us."

Reggie McNeal, *The Present Future*

"As a society, we are ill-equipped to consider
the differences and similarities among competing
religious traditions theologically."

Robert Wuthnow, *America and the
Challenges of Religious Diversity*

"I suggest that it is precisely religious changes
that are the most significant, and even the most
revolutionary, in the contemporary world. . . . We
are currently living through one of the transforming
moments in the history of religion worldwide."

Philip Jenkins, *The Next Christendom:
The Coming of Global Christianity*

This book began with observations that we live with a global awareness and new understandings of terrorism, war, and the meaning of security. We noted that as we look around the world we observe a shift among the nations that will influence the twenty-first century. The recognition that futurists are suggesting that China and India are the countries to watch for future economic influence and places like Nigeria, Brazil, and South Korea will be the sources of strength for a "new Christendom" call for us to think strategically about a global and future-directed role for Christian higher education. In order to think carefully about the future, we turn to the past for guidance.

Learning from William Carey

William Carey (1761–1834) is known as the father of modern missions. But when the twenty-five-year-old Carey began to talk about taking the gospel to the remotest parts of the earth, Baptist leaders in England replied, "Sit down, young man. If God wants to reach the heathen, He will do it without you." In response Carey wrote a brilliant treatise called *An Enquiry into the Obligations of Christians to Use Means for the Conversion of the Heathen*. Carey exhorted his readers to join him in expecting great things from God and attempting great things for God.

Carey invested his life in India. There this shoemaker was used of God to translate the gospel into the language of the people and bring a Christian presence to that distant land. In 1792 Carey and his colleagues formed the Particular Baptist Society for Propagating the Gospel Among the Heathen. Their adventure became the rallying point that pulled together both Particular and General Baptists, as well as Regular and Separate Baptists. This cooperative effort was significant in the life of British Baptists some two hundred years ago.

In the same way, Christian higher education can be a unifying and cooperative agent for the church at large in the twenty-first century. Nearly two centuries removed from the time of Carey, we face different tasks and different challenges, but we can learn from the two primary lessons in the life of William Carey. First, he believed that the church needed to take the gospel around the world. Second, he emphasized that God uses *means* to accomplish the spread of the gospel.

Christian higher education shares in the missional task by participating with others in the church of Jesus Christ to take the gospel around the world but also by recognizing that our unique role as educators is to use education as a means to accomplish that end. William Carey brilliantly argued that somehow within the mystery and providence of God it has been ordained that the Great Commission will be fulfilled through *means*, which includes the use of human instruments to accomplish God's purposes. In the changing world of the twenty-first century, it has never been more important to recognize education, and particularly higher education, as a unique agent to help carry forth Christ's commission.

To meet the challenges of a changing world, we should:

1. remind ourselves of the incredible changes in our global context;

2. recognize the importance of tolerance while rejecting the pressure to adopt a stance of religious pluralism, which downplays the uniqueness of the gospel message;

3. rethink the role of Christian higher education for es- tablishing a Christian presence in significant settings around the globe for the purpose of preevangelism;

4. realize the shift taking place in demographics and the expansion of Christianity in Asia and the Southern hemisphere;

5. reconsider the need to expand Christian higher edu- cation's international commitments to include inter- cultural opportunities as well; and

6. revisit William Carey's priorities for our day.

A Global World

We are living in an unprecedented age. Never before has the world seemingly been so accessible to all of us. Yet around the world we see poverty, terrorism, war, revolution, despair, destruction, and environmental challenges. As educators we live in the academic world, but our questions are not merely academic ones (in the negative sense of that word). We are not only educators but Christ-followers. We have eternity alive in our hearts, and we have been given the awesome priv- ilege of being involved in the kingdom work of our Lord Jesus Christ, a work which involves us in the pain of people around this globe and the promise of an eschatological hope. The two primary points of Carey's argument remain relevant for us. Yet the world in which we seek to apply those principles has significantly changed.

In the eighteenth century Carey's trip to India took almost twelve months. It was racked by the uncertainty of travel. The possibility of disease and death resulting from the lack of proper nutrition *en route* was part of the journey. A letter home telling of one's safe arrival might arrive two to three years after the original departure date. Today we live in a world where a trip from England to India can be made in a single day with meals, beverages, and movies provided. Telephones, e-mail, and text-messages let us confirm with loved ones that our trip was safe.

When Jesus commissioned His disciples to be witnesses in Jerusalem, Judea, and the uttermost parts of the world, the movement away from Jerusalem must have seemed endless. Modern transportation has brought the world next door, but those early disciples never dreamed of such a possibility. For them a trek to nearby Galilee took careful planning, the gathering of appropriate food and clothing, and preparation for business to continue as usual during a prolonged absence; but today we can travel twice that same distance in much less than one hour.

Communication in the eighteenth century depended on limited transportation, primarily by boat. But in the nineteenth century the first transatlantic telecommunication cable was successfully laid along the ocean floor. That step in the communication revolution set our globe on a course that will eventually seem to erase all distance. We can now send voice memos to hundreds of people simultaneously. Television networks compete for a two-to-five-second lead on breaking international stories.

We talk long-distance to friends on the other side of the ocean to see what the weather is like and to make sure they are doing fine. Thousands of phone calls and e-mails, as well as Internet calls using software like Skype, cross borders and oceans each hour, filled with conversations about the latest event in the life of the kids, a new recipe, discussion of the big game and sports statistics, second-guessing of the politicians, and information on covert military operations.

Distance does not affect things the way it once did. Board meetings take place through satellite-beamed conference calls where television images allow people to see each other as they talk. Fax machines, e-mails, and cell phones keep our world moving at breakneck speed. In recent years we have seen images of war and terroristic acts come right into our living rooms almost simultaneously with the events themselves.

Christian educators are more aware than ever that the world is a global place. Some economists speak of the formation of a global labor pool in which people around the world are competing for the same jobs. For example, it is possible today to buy a so-called foreign car made entirely in the United States. Toyota of Japan builds cars in Kentucky. At the same time, General Motors, Ford, and Daimler-Chrysler are selling cars that were assembled in South Korea, Mexico, or China.

Each year several hundred thousand immigrants move into major cities in this country, creating villages that make our nation's largest cities a virtual United Nations within themselves. What used to be unfamiliar distant faces, seen by North Americans only in *National Geographic* and on public television specials, are now the faces of our grocer, our mechanic, our students, and even our next-door neighbor.

In the age when many current faculty and administrators were growing up in the United States, we could have hardly imagined walking the pavement in Red Square in Moscow. My most vivid memory of that part of the world was Khrushchev banging on the platform, screaming, "We will bury you!" Today, like many others, I, on more than one occasion, have been to Russia. Moreover, several years ago, Mikhail Gorbachev spoke at Union University and spent an hour in conversation with me in my office. Such events were almost unimaginable to us just a few years ago.

In South America people are reading the French magazine *Elle* as well as the U.S.-produced *Better Homes and Gardens*. A trip to Latin America might include a meal of chicken chow mein while a visitor to Russia will find Russian youth wearing American designer jeans, eating French fries and Big Macs from McDonald's as they walk down the street. This is the changing world that Christian higher education has been called to serve.

Our natural tendency is to build walls around ourselves and protect our world from outsiders. Sometimes we are trying to protect the way things were. It would be like insisting on riding a horse, as John Wesley did, even though the automobile has been around for a hundred years. Learning to adapt to a changing world is more than a good idea; it is mandatory. We now live in a multiracial, multicolored, multiethnic context. We have the pleasure of seeing God's creation in all of its variety, which is a great gift from God.

New Opportunities for Christian Higher Education

As we contemplate our networked globe, we must recognize the growing opportunity this gives us for the advancement of the kingdom of God. A. T. Pierson, an important nineteenth-century missiologist, observed that the moment in which he lived presented both grand opportunity and great responsibility, a chance for glorious success or awful failure. Pierson's words could hardly be more appropriate for our day as well.

His generation could not have known the opportunities God would offer those of us living in the twenty-first century.

Every person created by the hand of God now lives within the reach of the gospel, be it through business, medicine, government, or, most importantly for us, education. Indeed, the current hour is unprecedented. The road is uncharted. Our opportunities are unmatched. We are called to be members of this global family as we step into the twenty-first century. The Global South may in fact become the majority players, as those in the West take a different role.

There is, however, another side to the story. The Christian voice is being discharged from its formerly privileged role in our Western society. During this transition we are discovering how accommodated we have become to the assumptions of the culture around us. If on the one hand we are jarred and shaken by the shift in the shrinking globe and the changes in the social landscape around us, we are faced on the other hand with a rude awakening to the fact that we unfortunately are more and more like the culture we now inhabit. Donald Posterski, in his work *Reinventing Evangelism: New Strategies for Presenting Christ in Today's World*, has put it well. He notes that instead of being in the world but not of the world, we have done the seemingly impossible; we have inverted Jesus' dictum and become of the world but not in the world.

One of the roles that Christian higher education can play is to help the church understand the need to live always between gospel and culture. We must recognize on the one hand the cultural dynamics that shape, and on the other hand we must listen to the gospel that calls us to know and value things in a different way.

One of the challenges for Christian higher education is to maintain a distinctive Christian presence that stands without reservation on the uniqueness of the gospel in contexts where the gospel is not well received. We cannot be forced into a false either/or choice between a supposed intolerant particularism or a supposed tolerant relativism. We *must* maintain a commitment to particularism while at the same time addressing the legitimate concerns for religious tolerance.

Christians around the world are unfortunately often described as intolerant or as persecuting or demeaning toward others. We can lead the way in simultaneously modeling a spirit of understanding along with an unapologetic commitment to the uniqueness of Jesus Christ and the gospel message. In this way Christian higher education has a unique opportunity to take the lead in establishing a credible Christian presence in places often hostile to the gospel.

What does all this have to do with the role of Christian higher education in the world? I would suggest a great deal. People cannot effectively respond to something they do not understand. One of our responsibilities in our educational role is to help our students and those with whom we partner around the world understand what religion teaches regarding the nature of ultimate reality and the fate of individuals at death. What is needed is to move the entire starting point of the conversation back one step.

Rather than beginning with any kind of confrontation, I believe it could be more fruitful first to address the assumption of the religious pluralists that all paths lead to the same destination. When the relativist recognizes that all religions cannot be true at the same time, he or she is generally more open to considering evidence for one particular faith. In this sense the role of Christ-centered higher education is not to do evangelistic church planting but first to carry out the role of preevangelism, maintaining a credible Christian presence in the world.

We can do this and remain committed to the legitimate concern that underlies the contemporary awareness of world religions. Buddhists, Hindus, Muslims, Jews, and Christians can and should live together without resorting to violence. Yet we recognize that world history does not offer a very encouraging picture in this regard. Our times are little better than those before us, but it is critical for Christians to affirm that we are against racism, bigotry, and other forms of intolerance that deny people the right to freely make their own decisions regarding matters of faith.

This may seem obvious, but many people falsely assume that Christians, particularly Christian particularists, do not believe in religious freedom. Yet pluralists need to recognize that it cannot be the case that Islamic monotheism and the plural gods of Hinduism are both correct. Thus when dealing with pluralists, it can be helpful to point out that most religions make both exclusive claims and diverse claims. Not just Christians are concerned about these vital matters. We can be champions of religious freedom while maintaining an unapologetic commitment to the exclusive claims of the gospel.

We also can help our friends see that it would be wrong to be tolerant about some things. A person who observes a rape and makes no attempt to stop it or report it would hardly be described as tolerant. Certain behaviors should not be tolerated because they are unhealthy for a society, and likewise certain beliefs have consequences for all eternity. We can also suggest that although truth is sometimes narrow, this does not make it intolerant. At times only one thing can be correct.

Such is the case with many important religious claims as well. We must distinguish between matters of preference and matters of truth. To suggest that crimson is my favorite color is a matter of preference. To suggest that Jesus Christ was a Jew who lived in Palestine during the early part of the first century is a matter of truth. To suggest that I enjoy ice cream is a matter of preference. To suggest that Jesus was executed on a cross, rose from the dead, and appeared to more than five hundred witnesses is a truth claim. It is helpful for us in our educational role to help people understand the difference between matters of preference and matters of truth. Each world religion makes statements about the nature of reality, and the truth or falsity of those statements *does matter*.

In light of the conflicting truth claims of various religions, it does not make sense to believe that all religions are equally valid. Although we live in an age when many think that no rational person could possibly believe that one religion alone is true while so many other religions exist and even thrive, we cannot immediately jump ship from the historical truth claims of the Christian faith.

Our role in higher education can be both apologetic as well as educational. This educational role may involve genuine preevangelism by being a Christian presence in the world. Our role is primarily to create an environment for spiritual progress and to engage in persuasive and authentic interaction with people while also demonstrating by our presence the credibility of the Christian faith.

Creating such an environment involves connecting the large unevangelized world eventually with the God of the

Bible. The role of Christian higher education is not so much that of shining a floodlight as it is lighting a candle. If someone is sitting in a dark room and you flip a switch that floods the room with light, the person in the room will wince and turn away from the source of the light, eyes shut tightly.

On the other hand, if you walk into a dark room with a candle, the person in the darkness will be attracted to the light. The unique role of Christ-centered higher education in a global context is the lighting of a candle in a dark world.

We understand that God is light and that in Him there is no darkness although we also understand that the world is separated from God and thus people are in darkness. Our role as educators then is to build ongoing relationships given time and opportunity. Hopefully such opportunities will help dispel misconceptions and break down barriers to the gospel message.

As we enter into friendships with unbelievers, we gain a platform through fostering relationships that will move us toward matters of the kingdom of God. There is certainly a place for direct communication.

In the Old Testament we find the use of direct communication in Leviticus 19: "Love your neighbor as yourself; I am the LORD" (v. 18). But in Luke 10, we see Jesus getting the same point across in an indirect manner when an expert in the law asks Him a question about loving his neighbor. In order to justify himself, the man asks, "Who is my neighbor that I am to love?" In reply Jesus tells the story of the good Samaritan. At the end of the story, He asks His questioner, "Which of the three men in the story was a neighbor to the man who fell into the hands of the robbers?" The legal expert answers,

"The one who had mercy on him." Jesus then tells him to go and do likewise.

By using an indirect and artful approach, Jesus was able to communicate His point to someone who was hostile to His message. Rather than wincing and turning away from the floodlight, the man got the point Jesus was making by use of the candle.

For this kind of interaction to take place, we must seek opportunities not only to speak but also to listen. Careful listening is an art. Before we can articulate the truths of God's kingdom, it is important that we learn to listen. As someone has well said, "How will they hear unless we learn to listen?"

The Future Work of Christian Higher Education

So where does this leave us? We live in a world where English is the new *Koine* in most discussions of globalization, but the Spanish language is most frequently spoken by Christians around the world. It leaves us in a context that points to the browning of Christianity and the movement of the Christian base toward Africa and South America. From a purely statistical point of view, Christianity in the twenty-first century will be a non-Western religion. Of course, the intervening work of God in another Great Awakening could change such directions, but the likely reality according to current trajectories is that the profile of Christianity in days ahead will be different.

The work of Penn State scholar Philip Jenkins underscores this reality. In *The Next Christendom: The Coming of Global Christianity*, and in his follow-up work *The New Faces of Christianity: Believing the Bible in the Global South*, Jenkins writes that in 1900 there were approximately ten million Christians in Africa. By 2000 there were 360 million. By 2025, conservative estimates see that number rising to over 630 million. Those same estimates put the number of Christians in Latin America in 2025 at 640 million and in Asia at 460 million. At that point the typical Christian will be a woman living in a Nigerian village or a Brazilian town.

What then must Christian higher education do if it hopes to contribute to the future of a global Christianity? The world is changing, and so must we. First and foremost we must remain anchored to Jesus Christ while geared to the times.

We must be willing to defer to non-Western opinions and ideas whenever our most basic convictions are not at stake. Western wealth and isolation have at times kept us from understanding the real issues of the "majority world" and those in the unevangelized belt. Similarly, we must recognize the importance that social justice plays in understanding the nature and work of God. One way of explaining the rise of liberation theology in Third World contexts is the church's failure to teach and practice justice. Our institutions need to engage in serious work that puts education, justice, and missions together as partners rather than competitors. Christian institutions of higher education that do not encourage students to wrestle with these shared issues are not preparing responsible Christ-followers for the twenty-first century.

The good news, however, is that young adults on our campuses easily accept the idea that Christians are to provide homes for the homeless and food for the hungry. They understand that they are to work for justice while simultaneously taking the good news of the gospel cross-culturally to new portions of the world. The generation of students currently on our campuses articulates the holistic call of the kingdom of God much more effectively and with greater zeal than those before them.

We must recognize that we live in a world with new faces, hard-to-pronounce names, and a rainbow of colors. This is our larger global family. Yet the family members don't seem to get along very well. Expanding global opportunities will increase our exposure to people who call themselves Christ-followers but whose ideas and backgrounds are different enough from ours to cause us possibly to withdraw rather than to pursue fellowship. We must recognize that what brings us together is not our homogeneous characteristics but our deep love for Jesus Christ, who has given us new life. Our lives then are to become an offering of thanks to Jesus, best expressed in lifestyles of compassion toward the least of these in our world. Our guide is Scripture itself, inspired by God the Holy Spirit.

We should assume our humble posture of listening to and learning from one another. All of us bring strengths and deficiencies to our shared work. Fear is a strong force in keeping us apart. A love for Jesus Christ and a desire to understand more of His truth can counter that fear and help us launch an exciting future for global Christian higher education in the days ahead.

While recognizing the implications for global education, it is important to acknowledge how few of us will actually relocate cross-culturally for long periods of time. Given this reality, perhaps we should think about our role not only as international work but also as intercultural work. The major cities of the United States are beginning to look as if the world has moved to our doorstep. Poverty, homelessness, drug abuse, and violence surround us. Our cities are multiethnic and intercultural. The call of Christian educators then must be expanded not only to have an international component but a growing intercultural component here in this country as well. Thus we must grapple with our insulation, a task which will require courageous decisions in the days ahead. We have the privilege of locally living out the global implications of our faith.

The missional and educational task of Christian higher education then is to develop global Christians on our campuses. We can take the leadership in our own situations, and we can join with others to forge relevant ties for our global work in the twenty-first century. We must not shy away from the task. We need to live as boldly as William Carey lived over two hundred years ago. Let us then expect great things from God; let us attempt great things for God. We need to ask for fresh eyes to see the potential role that Christian higher education has as the *means* for establishing a Christian presence in the world.

Let us therefore go forth in wisdom, humility, and confidence, recognizing the unique calling that is ours, ready to provide an answer for the hope that is in us through Jesus Christ our Lord (1 Pet 3:15). May God's favor and blessing rest on the future work of Christian higher education in this country and around the world.

Sources

Allen, Walter R., ed. *Higher Education in a Global Society*. Los Angeles: El Sevier, 2006.

Bedioko, Kwame. *Christianity in Africa*. Edinburgh: Edinburgh University Press, 1995.

Benveniste, Guy. *The Twenty-First Century Organization: Analyzing Current Trends and Imaging the Future.* San Francisco: Jossey-Bass, 1994.

Berger, Peter. *A Far Glory: The Quest for Faith in an Age of Credulity.* New York: Free Press, 1992.

Berger, Peter, et al., eds. *The Desecularization of the World: Resurgent Religion and World Politics.* Washington, DC: Ethics and Public Policy Center, 1999.

Bonk, Jonathan J. *Between Past and Future: Evangelical Mission Entering the Twenty-First Century.* Pasadena: William Carey Library, 2003.

Bruce, Steve. *Religion in the Modern World: From Cathedrals to Cults.* Oxford: Oxford University Press, 2005.

Carter, Stephen. *The Culture of Disbelief: How American Law and Politics Trivialize Religious Devotion.* New York: Basic Books, 1993.

Chandler, Russell. *Racing Toward 2001.* Grand Rapids: Zondervan, 1992.

Chia, Roland. *Hope for the World.* Downers Grove: InterVarsity, 2005.

Collins, Tim. *Good to Great.* New York: Harper Collins, 2001.

Conn, Harvie M. *Eternal Word and Changing Worlds: Theology, Anthropology, and Mission in Trialogue.* Grand Rapids: Zondervan, 1984.

Conyers, A. J. *The Long Truce: How Toleration Made the World Safe for Power and Profit.* Dallas, TX: Spence, 2001.

Davis, Derek H., and Barry Hankins, eds. *New Religious Movements and Religious Liberty in America.* Waco: Baylor University Press, 2003.

Dovre, Paul J. *The Future of Religious Colleges.* Grand Rapids: Eerdmans, 2002.

Gaede, Stan D. *When Tolerance Is No Virtue: Political Correctness, Multiculturalism and the Future of Truth and Justice*. Downers Grove: InterVarsity, 1993.

Gallup, Jr., George, and D. Michael Lindsay. *Surveying the Religious Landscape: Trends in U. S. Beliefs*. Harrisburg, PA: Morehouse, 1999.

George, Timothy. *Faithful Witness: The Life and Times of William Carey*. Birmingham, AL: Women's Missionary Union, 1991.

Heie, Harold. "Wanted: Christian Colleges for a Dynamic Evangelism." *Christian Scholars Review* 21, no. 3 (March 1992).

Jenkins, Philip. *The New Faces of Christianity: Believing the Bible in the Global South*. New York: Oxford University Press, 2006.

_____. *The Next Christendom: The Coming of Global Christianity*. Oxford: Oxford University Press, 2002.

Johnson, Ron. *How Will They Hear if We Don't Listen?* Nashville: Broadman & Holman, 1994.

McGrath, Alister. *Evangelicalism and the Future of Christianity*. Downers Grove: InterVarsity, 1995.

McNeal, Reggie. *The Present Future*. San Francisco: Jossey-Bass, 2003.

Netland, Harold A. *Encountering Religious Pluralism: The Challenge to Christian Faith and Mission*. Downers Grove: InterVarsity, 2001.

Newbigin, Leslie. *The Gospel in a Pluralist Society*. Grand Rapids: Eerdmans, 1989.

Posterski, Donald. *Reinventing Evangelism: New Strategies for Presenting Christ in Today's World*. Downers Grove: InterVarsity, 1989.

Robert, Dana Lee. *Occupy Until I Come: A. T. Pierson and the Evangelization of the World*. Grand Rapids: Eerdmans, 2003.

Sanneh, Lamin, and Joel Carpenter, eds. *The Changing Face of Christianity: Africa, the West, and the World*. Grand Rapids: Eerdmans, 2003.

White, James Emery. *Serious Times*. Downers Grove: InterVarsity, 2004.

Wolterstorff, Nicholas. *Educating for Shalom: Essays on Christian Higher Education*. Edited by Clarence Joldersma and Gloria Stronks. Grand Rapids: Eerdmans, 2004.

Wuthnow, Robert. *America and the Challenges of Religious Diversity*. Princeton: Princeton University Press, 2005.

_____. *The Restructuring of American Religion*. Princeton: Princeton University Press, 1988.

Wuthnow, Robert, and John H. Evans, eds. *The Quiet Hand of God: Faith Based Activism and the Public Role of Mainline Protestantism*. Berkeley: University of California Press, 2002.

A Bibliography for the Integration of Faith and Learning

"When you come bring the cloak . . . and the books,
especially the parchments."

2 Timothy 4:13 (NASB)

"Clearly one must read every good book
at least once every ten years."

C. S. Lewis, *The Letters of C. S.
Lewis to Arthur Greeves*

"All you need are a shelf full of books, a congenial friend
or two who can talk to you about your reading."

Susan Wise Bauer, *The
Well-Educated Mind*

"Christian education that is not intellectually demanding
may be living on borrowed time."

Carl F. H. Henry, *Twilight
of a Great Civilization*

The integration of faith and learning is one of the most important and distinctive characteristics of Christian higher education. Education at a Christian university involves more than the delivery of content in the classroom in an effective way. It also involves helping students learn to see the world through the lenses of a Christian worldview. Other distinctives include providing competencies in one's chosen field of study and helping to shape character for life and vocation.

Faculties at Christian universities must be committed to loving God with their minds, the essence of what it means to be a Great Commandment university. Faculty, staff, and students must learn to think Christianly. This commitment involves integrating faith and knowledge in all disciplines.

This bibliographical tool has been compiled to help accomplish these goals. Our hope is that many will find it helpful as they seek to think holistically about various subjects from a Christian perspective.

Not every book in the bibliography is written from a faith perspective. Yet even those books help us understand the issues and challenges facing Christian institutions as they move into what many are calling a post-Christian cultural context. Our prayer is that God will use this bibliography as a tool to advance the work of Christian higher education.

Periodicals/Tapes/Organizations

Books and Culture
Christian Research Journal
Christian Scholar's Review
Christianity Today

Faculty Dialogue

First Things

Kairos Journal

Journal for the Institute for Christian Leadership

Mars Hill Tapes

Regeneration Quarterly

Touchstone

World

(p) = periodical   (o) = organization

Education

(p) *Christian Education Journal*

(o) North American Professors of Christian Education

History

(o) Conference on Faith and History

(p) *Fides et Historia*

Language and International Studies

(o) Christian Educators in Teachers of English to Speakers of Other Languages

(p) Language, Linguistics and International Studies

(p) *NACFLA Proceedings Journal Studies in Third World Societies*

(o) Network of Christian Anthropologists

(o) North American Association of Christian Foreign Language and Literature Faculty

(o) Teachers of English to Speakers of Other Languages

Visual Arts, Music, and Culture

(o) Christian Fellowship of Art and Music Composers

(o) Christians in the Arts Networking

(o) Christians in the Visual Arts

(o) Christian Performing Artists Fellowship

(p) *A Journal of the Arts and Religion*

Communication Arts

(o) Christians in the Theatre Arts

(o) International Christian Visual Media Association

(p) *Journal of Religion and Communication*

(o) Religious Communication Association

(o) Religious Speech Communication Association

Literature

(p) *Christianity and Literature*

(o) The Conference on Christianity and Literature

Nursing, Health Care, and Biomedical Ethics

(o) Baptist Medical-Dental Fellowship

(o) Baptist Nursing Fellowship

(o) The Center for Bioethics and Human Dignity

(o) Christian Medical and Dental Society

(o) Christian Pharmacists Fellowship International

(p) *Christianity and Pharmacy*

(p) *Ethics and Medicine*

(p) *Health Wise*

(p) *Journal of Christian Nursing*

(o) Nurses Christian Fellowship

Business and Economics

(o) Association of Christian Economists

(p) *Business Reform*

(o) Christian Business Faculty Association

Law and Political Science

(o) Christians in Political Science

(o) Christian Legal Society

(p) *Notre Dame Journal of Law, Ethics and Public Policy*

Mathematics

(o) Association of Christians in Mathematical Sciences

Philosophy/Ethics

(o) Evangelical Philosophical Society

(p) *Faith and Philosophy*

(p) *Philosophia Christi*

(o) Society of Christian Ethics

(o) Society of Christian Philosophers

Psychology

(o) American Association of Christian Counselors

(o) American Psychological Association

(o) Christian Association for Psychological Studies

(p) *Christian Counseling Today*

(p) *Journal of Psychology and Theology*

Science and Environment

(o) Affiliation of Christian Biologists

(o) Affiliation of Christian Geologists

(o) American Scientific Affiliation

(o) Association of Christian Engineers and Scientists

(o) Christian Environmental Association

(o) Christian Society of the Green Cross

(p) *Creation Care*

(o) Creation Research Society

(p) *Creation Research Society Quarterly*

(p) *Green Cross: A Christian Environmental Quarterly*

(p) *Journal of "Christians in Science"*

(p) *Perspectives on Science and Christian Faith*

(p) *Science and Christian Belief*

(p) *Teachers in Focus Environmental Studies*

Sociology/Social Work

(o) Association of Christians Teaching Sociology

(o) Christian Sociological Society

(p) *Christian Sociologist*

(o) North American Association of Christians in Social Work

(p) *Social Work and Christianity*

Theology/Biblical Studies

(p) *Bibliotheca Sacra*

(p) *Calvin Theological Journal*

(p) *Catholic Biblical Quarterly*

(o) Christian Theological Research Fellowship

(o) Evangelical Theological Society

(o) Evangelical Theology Group of the American Academy of Religion

(p) *Faith and Mission*

(o) Institute for Biblical Research

(p) *Journal of IBR*

(p) *Journal of the Evangelical Theological Society*

(p) *Southern Baptist Journal of Theology*

(p) *Southwestern Journal of Theology*

(p) *Theology Today*

(p) *Tyndale Bulletin*

Christian Foundations and Worldview

Blamires, Harry. *The Christian Mind*. Ann Arbor: Servant, 1978.

_____. *A God Who Acts*. Ann Arbor: Servant, 1957.

_____. *Recovering the Christian Mind*. Downers Grove: InterVarsity, 1988.

Carson, Donald A. *The Gagging of God: Christianity Confronts Pluralism*. Grand Rapids: Zondervan, 1996.

Chesterton, G. R. *Orthodoxy*. San Francisco: Ignatius, 1995. Originally published 1908.

Colson, Charles, with Anne Morse. *Burden of Truth: Defending Truth in an Age of Unbelief*. Wheaton: Tyndale, 1997.

_____, with Nancy Pearcey. *How Now Shall We Live?* Wheaton: Tyndale, 1999.

Dockery, David S., and Gregory A. Thornbury, eds. *Shaping a Christian Worldview*. Nashville: Broadman & Holman, 2002.

Dudley-Smith, Timothy, ed. *Authentic Christianity: From the Writings of John Stott*. Downers Grove: InterVarsity, 1996.

Ellul, Jacques. *The Presence of the Kingdom*. Translated by Olive Wyon. New York: Seabury, 1967.

Guinness, Os. *The American Hour: A Time of Reckoning and the Once and Future Role of Faith*. New York: Free Press, 1993.

_____. *The Gravedigger Files*. Downers Grove: InterVarsity, 1983.

Helm, Paul. *Faith and Understanding*. Grand Rapids: Eerdmans, 1997.

Henry, Carl F. H. *The Christian Mindset in a Secular Culture*. Portland: Multnomah, 1984.

Holmes, Arthur F. *All Truth Is God's Truth*. Downers Grove: InterVarsity, 1977.

_____. *Contours of a Worldview*. Grand Rapids: Eerdmans, 1983.

_____. *Fact, Value and God*. Grand Rapids: Eerdmans, 1997.

_____. *The Making of a Christian Mind: A Christian World View and the Academic Enterprise*. Downers Grove: InterVarsity, 1985.

Kuyper, Abraham. 1898 Stone Lectures, Princeton University. In *Creating a Christian Worldview*. Compiled by Peter S. Heslam. Grand Rapids: Eerdmans, 1998.

Ladd, George E. *The Pattern of New Testament Truth*. Grand Rapids: Eerdmans, 1968.

Lewis, C. S. *Mere Christianity*. New York: Macmillan, 1943.

McGrath, Alister. *Christianity's Dangerous Idea: The Origins and Transformation of Protestantism, 1500–2000*. San Francisco: Harper San Francisco, 2007.

Machen, J. Gresham. *What Is Christianity?* Edited by Ned B. Stonehouse. Grand Rapids: Eerdmans, 1951.

Marshall, Paul, et al. *Stained Glass: Worldviews and Social Science*. Lanham, MD: University Press of America, 1989.

Moreland, J. P. *Love Your God with All Your Mind*. Colorado Springs: NavPress, 1997.

_____, and Kal Nielsen. *Does God Exist?* Buffalo: Prometheus, 1993.

_____, and William Lane Craig. *Philosophical Foundations for a Christian Worldview*. Downers Grove: InterVarsity, 2003.

Nagle, David. *Worldview: The History of a Concept*. Grand Rapids: Eerdmans, 2002.

Newbigin, Leslie. *Foolishness to the Greeks: The Gospel and Western Culture*. Grand Rapids: Eerdmans, 1986.

_____. *The Gospel in a Pluralist Society*. Grand Rapids: Eerdmans, 1989.

Noll, Mark, and David Wells, eds. *Christian Faith and Practice in the Modern World*. Grand Rapids: Eerdmans, 1987.

Orr, James. *The Christian View of God and the World*. Grand Rapids: Eerdmans, 1954. Originally published 1891.

Poe, Harry L. *The Gospel and Its Meaning*. Grand Rapids: Zondervan, 1996.

Pratt, Richard. *Every Thought Captive*. Phillipsburg, NJ: Presbyterian & Reformed, 1979.

Reeves, Thomas C. *The Empty Church: The Suicide of Liberal Christianity*. New York: Free Press, 1996.

Schaeffer, Francis. *The God Who Is There*. Downers Grove: InterVarsity, 1968.

Schlossberg, Herbert. *Idols for Destruction*. Wheaton: Crossway, 1990.

Sire, James W. *Naming the Elephant: Worldview as a Concept*. Downers Grove: InterVarsity, 2004.

_____. *The Universe Next Door: A Basic Worldview Catalog*. Rev. ed. Downers Grove: InterVarsity, 1997.

Stott, John R. W. *Your Mind Matters*. Downers Grove: InterVarsity, 1972.

Walsh, Brian J., and J. Richard Middleton. *The Transforming Vision: Shaping a Christian Worldview*. Downers Grove: InterVarsity, 1984.

Walters, Albert. *Creation Regained*. Grand Rapids: Eerdmans, 1985.

Wuthnow, Robert. *Christianity in the Twenty-First Century: Reflections on the Challenges Ahead*. New York: Oxford University Press, 1995.

Faith and Reason

Boa, Kenneth D., and Robert M. Bowman Jr. *Faith Has Its Reasons.* Waynesboro, GA: Paternoster, 2006.

Burson, Scott F., and Jerry L. Walls. *C. S. Lewis and Francis Schaeffer: Lessons for a New Century from the Most Influential Apologists of Our Time.* Downers Grove: InterVarsity, 1998.

Colson, Charles. *Burden of Truth: Defending the Truth in an Age of Unbelief.* Wheaton: Tyndale, 1997.

Craig, William Lane. *Reasonable Faith.* Wheaton: Crossway, 1994.

Delaney, C. F., ed. *Rationality and Religious Belief.* Notre Dame: University of Notre Dame Press, 1979.

Evans, C. Stephen. *Why Believe? Reason and Mystery as Pointers to God.* Rev. ed. Grand Rapids: Eerdmans, 1996.

George, Robert P. *The Clash of Orthodoxies: Law, Religion, and Morality in Crisis.* Wilmington, DE: ISI Books, 2001.

Johnson, Phillip E. *Reason in the Balance.* Downers Grove: InterVarsity, 1995.

Kreeft, Peter, and Ronald K. Tacelli. *Handbook of Christian Apologetics.* Downers Grove: InterVarsity, 1994.

McGrath, Alister. *Intellectuals Don't Need God and Other Modern Myths.* Grand Rapids: Zondervan, 1993.

_____. *The Twilight of Atheism: The Rise and Fall of Disbelief in the Modern World.* London: Rider, 2004.

Migliore, Daniel. *Faith Seeking Understanding.* Grand Rapids: Eerdmans, 2004.

Nash, Ronald. *Faith and Reason.* Grand Rapids: Zondervan, 1988.

Olson, Roger E. *The Mosaic of Christian Beliefs.* Downers Grove: InterVarsity, 2002.

Plantinga, Alvin, and Nicholas Wolterstorff, eds. *Faith and Rationality: Reason and Belief in God*. Notre Dame: University of Notre Dame Press, 1983.

Poe, Harry Lee, and Rebecca Whitten Poe, eds. *C. S. Lewis Remembered: Collected Reflections of Students, Friends and Colleagues*. Grand Rapids: Zondervan, 2006.

Schaeffer, Francis. *Escape from Reason*. Downers Grove: InterVarsity, 1968.

Wolterstorff, Nicholas. *Reason within the Bounds of Religion*. Grand Rapids: Eerdmans, 1984.

Theological Foundations

Barth, Karl. *Church Dogmatics*. Edited and translated by Geoffrey Bromiley, Thomas Forsythe Torrance, G. T. Thompson, and Harold Knight. 14 vols. Edinburgh: T&T Clark, reprint 2004.

_____. *Evangelical Theology*. Translated by Grover Foley. Grand Rapids: Eerdmans, 1983.

Bloesch, Donald G. *Essentials of Evangelical Theology*. 2 vols. San Francisco: Harper & Row, 1979.

Boice, James. *Foundations of the Christian Faith*. Downers Grove: InterVarsity, 1986.

Calvin, John. *Institutes of the Christian Religion*. 2 vols. Editor John T. McNeil. Translated by Ford Lewis Battles. Library of Christian Classics. Philadelphia: Westminster, 1960.

Charry, Ellen, ed. *Inquiring after God: Classic and Contemporary Readings*. Oxford: Blackwell, 1999.

Conyers, A. J. *A Basic Christian Theology*. Nashville: Broadman & Holman, 1995.

Dockery, David S. *Christian Scripture*. Nashville: Broadman & Holman, 1995.

_____, ed. *New Dimensions in Evangelical Thought*. Downers Grove: InterVarsity, 1998.

Elwell, Walter A., ed. *Evangelical Dictionary of Theology*. Grand Rapids: Baker, 1984.

Erickson, Millard J. *Christian Theology*. Rev. ed. Grand Rapids: Baker, 1998.

Ferguson, Sinclair, David Wright and J. I. Packer, eds. *New Dictionary of Theology*. Downers Grove: InterVarsity, 1988.

Frame, John. *Salvation Belongs to the Lord: An Introduction to Systematic Theology*. Phillipsburg, NJ: P&R Publishing, 2006.

Garrett, James Leo. *Systematic Theology*. 2 vols. Grand Rapids: Eerdmans, 1995.

Geisler, Norman. *Systematic Theology*. 4 vols. Minneapolis: Bethany, 2005.

George, Timothy, and David S. Dockery. *Theologians of the Baptist Tradition*. Nashville: Broadman & Holman, 2001.

Grenz, Stanley J. *Theology for the Community of God*. Nashville: Broadman & Holman, 1994.

Grudem, Wayne. *Systematic Theology*. Grand Rapids: Zondervan, 1994.

Henry, Carl F. H. *God, Revelation and Authority*. 6 vols. Waco: Word, 1976.

House, Paul R. *Old Testament Theology*. Downers Grove: InterVarsity, 1998.

Johnson, Alan F., and Robert E. Webber. *What Christians Believe*. Grand Rapids: Zondervan, 1989.

Lewis, Gordon, and Bruce Demarest. *Integrative Theology*. Grand Rapids: Zondervan, 1996.

McGrath, Alister. *Christian Theology*. Oxford: Blackwell, 1994.

Oden, Thomas. *Systematic Theology*. Vol. 1, *The Living God*. San Francisco: Harper & Row, 1987.

Packer, J. I. *Concise Theology: A Guide to Historic Christian Beliefs.* Wheaton: Tyndale, 1993.

_____. *Knowing God.* Downers Grove: InterVarsity, 1973.

Packer, J. I., and Thomas C. Oden. *One Faith: The Evangelical Consensus.* Downers Grove: InterVarsity, 2004.

Tabb, Mark. *Theology: Think for Yourself about What You Believe.* Colorado Springs: NavPress, 2006.

Thielman, Frank. *New Testament Theology.* Grand Rapids: Zondervan, 2005.

Basic Biblical Studies

Arnold, Bill T., and Bryan E. Beyer. *Encountering the Old Testament: A Christian Survey.* Grand Rapids: Baker, 1999.

Black, D. A., and David S. Dockery. *Interpreting the New Testament.* Nashville: Broadman & Holman, 2001.

Bromiley, Geoffrey, ed. *The International Standard Bible Encyclopedia.* Grand Rapids: Eerdmans, 1988.

Brown, Colin, ed. *Dictionary of New Testament Theology.* 3 vols. Grand Rapids: Zondervan, 1978.

Butler, Trent C., ed. *Holman Bible Dictionary.* Nashville: Holman, 1991.

Carson, D. A., and D. J. Moo. *An Introduction to the New Testament.* Grand Rapids: Zondervan, 2005.

Dockery, David S., ed. *Holman Bible Handbook.* Nashville: Holman, 1992.

_____, ed. *Holman Concise Bible Commentary.* Nashville: Holman, 1998.

_____, K. A. Mathews, and R. B. Sloan, eds. *Foundations for Biblical Interpretation.* Nashville: Broadman & Holman, 1994.

Elwell, Walter, ed. *Baker Encyclopedia of the Bible*. Grand Rapids: Baker, 1988.

_____, ed. *Evangelical Commentary of the Bible*. Grand Rapids: Baker, 1989.

_____, ed. *Evangelical Dictionary of Biblical Theology*. Grand Rapids: Baker, 1996.

Fee, Gordon D., and Douglas Stuart. *How to Read the Bible for All Its Worth*. Grand Rapids: Zondervan, 1981.

Green, Joel B., Scot McKnight, and I. Howard Marshall, eds. *Dictionary of Jesus and the Gospels*. Downers Grove: InterVarsity, 1992.

Hawthorne, Gerald, Ralph P. Martin, and Daniel G. Reid, eds. *Dictionary of Paul and His Letters*. Downers Grove: InterVarsity, 1993.

Martin, Ralph P., and Peter Davids, eds. *Dictionary of the Later New Testament and Its Developments*. Downers Grove: InterVarsity, 1997.

Ryken, Leland, and Tremper Longman III, eds. *A Complete Literary Guide to the Bible*. Grand Rapids: Zondervan, 1993.

Ryken, Leland, et al., eds. *Dictionary of Biblical Imagery*. Downers Grove: InterVarsity, 1998.

VanGemeren, Willem A. *New International Dictionary of Old Testament Theology and Exegesis*. 5 vols. Grand Rapids: Zondervan, 1997.

Bible Commentary Series

Baker Exegetical Commentary (Baker)

The Bible Speaks Today (*InterVarsity*)

Expositor's Bible Commentary (Zondervan)

IVP New Testament Commentary (InterVarsity)

New American Commentary (B&H)

New International Commentary on the New Testament (Eerdmans)

New International Commentary on the Old Testament (Eerdmans)

New Testament Commentary (Baker)

NIV Application Commentary (Zondervan)

Tyndale Commentary (*InterVarsity*)

Word Biblical Commentary (*Word/Nelson*)

Visual Arts, Music and Culture

Bailey, A. E. *The Gospel in Hymns*. New York: Charles Scribner, 1950.

Best, Harold. *Music Through the Eyes of Faith*. San Francisco: Harper, 1993.

Brand, Hilary, and Adrienne Chaplin. *Art and Soul: Signposts for Christians in the Arts*. Carlisle, CA: Piguant, 2001.

Briner, Bob. *Roaring Lambs: A Gentle Plan to Radically Change Your World*. Grand Rapids: Zondervan, 1993.

Bustard, Ned, ed. *It Was Good: Making Art to the Glory of God*. Baltimore: Square Halo, 2007.

Cowan, Louise, and Os Guinness, eds. *Invitation to the Classics*. Grand Rapids: Baker, 1998.

Dillenberger, John. *Style and Content in Christian Art*. London: Books on Demand, 1986.

Dyrness, William. *A Visual Faith: Art, Theology and Worship in Dialogue*. Grand Rapids: Baker, 2001.

Gaebelein, Frank Ely. *The Christian, The Arts, and Truth: Regaining the Vision of Greatness*. Grand Rapids: Zondervan, 1985.

Hospers, John. *Understanding the Arts*. Englewood Cliffs, NJ: Prentice-Hall, 1982.

Johnston, R. K. *Reel Spirituality: Theology and Film in Dialogue.* Grand Rapids: Baker, 2000.

Jones, Paul S. *Singing and Making Music.* Phillipsburg, NJ: P&R, 2006.

Kerman, Joseph. *Contemplating Music: Challenges to Musicology.* Cambridge, MA: Harvard University Press, 1985.

Lasch, Christopher. *The Culture of Narcissism.* New York: Warner, 1979.

_____. *The True and Only Heaven: Progress and Its Critics.* New York: Norton, 1991.

L'Engle, Madeline. *Walking on Water: Reflections on Faith and Art.* Wheaton: Harold Shaw, 1980.

Marsh, Clive, and Gaye Ortiz, eds. *Explorations in Theology and Film: Movies and Meaning.* Oxford: Blackwell, 1997.

Myers, Kenneth A. *All God's Children and Blue Suede Shoes.* Wheaton: Crossway, 1989.

Postman, Neil. *Amusing Ourselves to Death.* New York: Penguin, 1985.

_____. *Technopoly: The Surrender of Culture to Technology.* New York: Vintage, 1993.

Romanowski, William D. *Pop Culture Wars: Religion and the Role of Entertainment in American Life.* Downers Grove: InterVarsity, 1996.

Rookmaaker, Hans. *Modern Art and the Death of Culture.* Wheaton: Crossway, 1994.

Routley, Erik. *Our Lives Be Praise.* Carol Steam, IL: Hope, 1990.

Ryken, Leland, ed. *The Christian Imagination: Essays on Literature and the Arts.* Grand Rapids: Baker, 1981.

_____, *Culture in Christian Perspective.* Portland: Multnomah, 1986.

Ryken, Philip Graham. *Art for God's Sake: A Call to Recover the Arts.* Phillipsburg, NJ: P&R, 2006.

Sayers, Dorothy. *The Mind of the Maker*. San Francisco: Harper & Row, 1987.

Schaeffer, Francis. *Art and the Bible*. Downers Grove: InterVarsity, 1973.

_____. *How Should We Then Live: The Rise and Decline of Western Thought and Culture*. Old Tappan: Revell, 1976.

Stone, Bryan P. *Faith and Film: Theological Themes at the Cinema*. St. Louis: Chalice, 2000.

Turner, Steve. *Imagine: A Vision for Christians in the Arts*. Downers Grove: InterVarsity, 2001.

Veith, Gene Edward, Jr. *Painters of Faith*. Washington, DC: Regnery, 2001.

_____. *Postmodern Times: A Christian Guide to Contemporary Culture*. Wheaton: Crossway, 1994.

_____. *State of the Arts: From Bezalel to Mapplethorpe*. Wheaton: Crossway, 1991.

Westermeyer, Paul. *The Church Musician*. Minneapolis: Augsburg/Fortress, 1997.

Wolterstorff, Nicholas. *Art in Action: Toward a Christian Aesthetic*. Grand Rapids: Eerdmans, 1980.

_____. *Works and Worlds of Art*. New York: Oxford University Press, 1980.

Wright, Craig. *The Maze and the Warrior: Symbols in Architecture, Theology, and Music*. Cambridge, MA: Harvard University Press, 2001.

Business and Economics

Alford, Helen J., and Michael Naughton. *Managing as if Faith Mattered*. Notre Dame: University of Notre Dame Press, 2001.

Beauchamp, Tom L., and Norman E. Bowie. *Ethical Theory and Business.* Englewood Cliffs, NJ: Prentice-Hall, 1997.

Beckett, John D. *Loving Monday: Succeeding in Business without Selling Your Soul.* Downers Grove: InterVarsity, 1998.

Beisner, E. Calvin. *Prospects for Growth: A Biblical View of Population, Resources, and the Future.* Wheaton: Crossway, 1990.

_____. *Prosperity and Poverty: The Compassionate Use of Resources in a World of Scarcity.* Wheaton: Crossway, 1988.

Brookes, Warren T. *The Economy in Mind.* New York: Universe, 1993.

Burkett, Larry. *Business by the Book.* Nashville: Nelson, 1998.

Chewning, Richard. *Biblical Principles and Economics.* Colorado Springs: NavPress, 1989.

_____, John W. Eby, and Shirley J. Roels. *Business through the Eyes of Faith.* San Francisco: Harper & Row, 1990.

Childs, James M., Jr. *Ethics in Business: Faith at Work.* Minneapolis: Fortress, 1995.

Chilton, David. *Productive Christians in an Age of Guilt Manipulators.* Tyler, TX: Institute for Christian Economics, 1985.

Clouse, Robert, ed. *Wealth and Poverty: Four Christians' Views of Economics.* Downers Grove: InterVarsity, 1984.

Cramp, A. B. *Notes toward a Christian Critique of Secular Economic Theory.* Toronto: Institute for Christian Studies, 1975.

Ellul, Jacques. *Money and Power.* Translated by LaVonne Neff. Downers Grove: InterVarsity, 1984.

Gay, Craig M. *With Liberty and Justice for Whom?* Grand Rapids: Eerdmans, 1991.

Gilder, George. *Wealth and Poverty.* San Francisco: ICS, 1993.

Griffiths, Brian. *The Creation of Wealth*. Downers Grove: InterVarsity, 1985.

Halterman, James. *The Clashing Worlds of Economics and Faith*. Scottsdale, PA: Herald, 1995.

Hill, Alexander. *Just Business: Christian Ethics for the Marketplace*. Downers Grove: InterVarsity, 1997.

Houck, John, and Oliver Williams, eds. *The Judeo-Christian Vision and the Modern Corporation*. Notre Dame: University of Notre Dame Press, 1982.

Nash, Ronald H. *Social Justice and the Christian Hope*. Milford, MI: Mott, 1983.

Novak, Michael. *Business as Calling: Work and the Examined Life*. New York: Free Press, 1996.

Olasky, Marvin N., ed. *Freedom, Justice and Hope*. Wheaton: Crossway, 1988.

_____. *The Tragedy of American Compassion*. Washington, D.C.: Regnery, 1992.

Owensby, Walter. *Economics for Prophets*. Grand Rapids: Eerdmans, 1989.

Rae, Scott, and Kenman Wong. *Beyond Integrity: A Judeo-Christian Approach to Business Ethics*. Grand Rapids: Zondervan, 1996.

Schaeffer, Francis. *Death in the City*. Downers Grove: InterVarsity, 1969.

Schumacher, E. F. *Small Is Beautiful*. San Francisco: Harper & Row, 1989.

Sider, Ron. *Rich Christians in an Age of Hunger*. Dallas: Word, 1990.

Stackhouse, Max. *Public Theology and Political Economy: Christian Stewardship in Modern Society*. Grand Rapids: Eerdmans, 1987.

Storkey, Alan. *Transforming Economics: A Christian Way to Employment.* London: SPCK, 1986.

Ward, Benjamin. *The Ideal Worlds of Economics: Liberal, Radical and Conservative Economic Worldviews.* New York: Basic, 1979.

Communication Arts

Bachman, John W. *Media, Wasteland or Wonderland.* Minneapolis: Augsburg, 1984.

Fore, W. F. *Television and Religion: The Shaping of Faith, Values and Culture.* Minneapolis: Augsburg, 1987.

Goethals, Gregor. *The TV Ritual: Worship at the Video Altar.* Boston: Beacon, 1981.

Griffin, Emory A. *The Mind Changers: The Art of Christian Persuasion.* Wheaton: Tyndale, 1976.

Horsfield, Peter G. *Religious Television: The American Experience.* New York: Longman, 1984.

Lewis, Todd. *RT: A Reader's Theatre Ministry.* Kansas City: Lillenas, 1988.

Lyon, David. *The Information Society.* New York: Basil Blackwell, 1988.

Nash, Tom. *The Christian Communicator's Handbook.* Wheaton: Victor, 1995.

Nelson, John W. *Your God Is Alive and Well and Appearing in Popular Culture.* Philadelphia: Westminster, 1976.

Olasky, Marvin. *Prodigal Press: The Anti-Christian Bias of the American News Media.* Wheaton: Crossway, 1988.

_____. *Telling the Truth: How to Revitalize Christian Journalism.* Wheaton: Crossway, 1996.

Pippert, Wesley G. *An Ethics of News: A Reporter's Search for Truth*. Washington, D.C.: Georgetown University Press, 1989.

Schultze, Quentin J. *American Evangelicals and the Mass Media*. Grand Rapids: Zondervan, 1990.

_____. *Television: Manna from Hollywood*. Grand Rapids: Zondervan, 1986.

Sommerville, John. *How the News Makes Us Dumb: The Death of Wisdom in an Information Society*. Downers Grove: InterVarsity, 1999.

Strom, Bill. *More Than Talk: Communication Studies and the Christian Faith*. Dubuque: Kendall/Hunt Publishing Co., 1996.

Vos, Nelvin. *The Great Pendulum of Becoming: Images in Modern Drama*. Grand Rapids: Eerdmans, 1981.

Educational and Spiritual Formation

Adler, Mortimer J., and Charles Van Doren. *How to Read a Book*. New York: Simon & Schuster, 1972.

Augustine. *The Confessions*. New York: Doubleday, 1960. Written c. AD 397–401.

Bauer, Susan Wise. *The Well-Educated Mind: A Guide to the Classical Education You Never Had*. New York: Norton, 2003.

Bernard of Clairvaux. *The Love of God and Spiritual Friendship*. Edited by James A. Houston. Portland: Multnomah, reprint 1983.

Bridges, Jerry. *The Pursuit of Holiness*. Colorado Springs: NavPress, 1978.

Buechner, Frederick. *Now and Then*. San Francisco: Harper Collins, 1991.

Colson, Charles, ed. *Loving God*. Grand Rapids: Zondervan, 1987.

Foster, Richard J. *Celebration of Discipline*. San Francisco: HarperSanFrancisco, 1994.

Garber, Steven. *The Fabric of Faithfulness*. Downers Grove: InterVarsity, 1996.

Guinness, Os. *The Call: Finding and Fulfilling the Central Purpose of Your Life*. Nashville: Word, 1998.

Gushee, David P., and Walter Jackson, eds. *Preparing for Christian Ministry: An Evangelical Approach*. Wheaton: Victor/ BridgePoint, 1996.

Holmes, Arthur F. *Shaping Character*. Grand Rapids: Eerdmans, 1991.

Hunt, T. W. *The Mind of Christ*. Nashville: Broadman & Holman, 1997.

Kempis, Thomas à. *The Imitation of Christ*. New York: Grosset, [n.d.]. First published about 1440.

Law, William. *A Serious Call to a Devout and Holy Life*. Grand Rapids: Eerdmans, 1966. First published 1728.

Lawrence, Brother. *The Practice of the Presence of God*. Uhrichsville, OH: Barbour, 1998. First published about 1695.

Lewis, C. S. *God in the Dock*. Grand Rapids: Eerdmans, reprint 1994. First published 1970.

_____. *Surprised by Joy*. New York: Harcourt Brace, 1956.

_____. *The Weight of Glory and Other Addresses*. New York: Macmillan, 1980.

Longman, Tremper, III. *Reading the Bible with Mind and Heart*. Colorado Springs: NavPress, 1997.

Martin, Warren Bryan. *College of Character*. San Francisco: Jossey-Bass, 1984.

McDonald, Gordon. *Ordering Your Private World*. Nashville: Oliver-Nelson, 1985.

Meilaender, Gilbert. *Friendship*. Notre Dame: University of Notre Dame Press, 1981.

Nouwen, Henri M. *Reaching Out*. Garden City, NY: Doubleday, 1966.

_____. *The Way of the Heart*. New York: Ballantine, 1981.

Packer, J. I. *Knowing God*. Downers Grove: InterVarsity, 1973.

Palmer, Parker. *To Know as We Are Known: The Spirituality of Education*. San Francisco: HarperSanFrancisco, 1993.

Piper, John. *Desiring God*. Portland: Multnomah Press, revised 1996.

_____. *Let the Nations Be Glad: The Supremacy of God in Missions*. Grand Rapids: Baker, 1993.

Sire, James W. *Discipleship of the Mind*. Downers Grove: InterVarsity, 1990.

_____. *How to Read Slowly*. Wheaton: Harold Shaw, 1978.

Steele, Les. *On the Way: A Practical Theology of Christian Formation*. Grand Rapids: Baker, 1990.

Stott, John R. W. *Your Mind Matters*. Downers Grove: InterVarsity, 1973.

Tozer, A. W. *The Attributes of God*. Camp Hill, PA: Christian Publications, 1997.

_____. *The Pursuit of God*. Harrisburg, PA: Christian Publications, 1982.

Veith, Gene Edward. *Loving God with All Your Mind*. Westchester: Crossway, 1987.

Wesley, John. *A Plain Account of Christian Perfection*. London: Epworth, reprint 1952.

Whitney, Donald S. *Spiritual Disciplines for the Christian Life*. Colorado Springs: NavPress, 1997.

Wilberforce, William. *Real Christianity*. Portland: Multnomah, reprint 1982.

Willard, Dallas. *In Search of Guidance*. San Francisco: HarperSanFrancisco, 1993.

_____. *The Spirit of the Disciplines*. San Francisco: HarperSanFrancisco, 1990.

Higher Education

Alken, Henry David. *Predicament of the University*. Bloomington: Indiana University Press, 1971.

Anderson, Chris. *Teaching as Believing: Faith in the University*. Waco: Baylor University Press, 2004.

Benne, Robert. *Quality with Soul*. Grand Rapids: Eerdmans, 2001.

Blamires, Harry. *Repair the Ruins: Reflections on Educational Matters from a Christian Point of View*. London: Geoffrey Bles, 1950.

Bloom, Allan. *The Closing of the American Mind*. New York: Simon & Schuster, 1987.

Brill, E. H. *Religion and the Rise of the University*. Ann Arbor, MI: University Microfilms, 1970.

Budde, Michael L., and John Wright. *Conflicting Allegiances: The Church-Based University in a Liberal Democratic Society*. Grand Rapids: Brazos, 2004.

Bunting, Josiah. *An Education for Our Time*. Washington, DC: Regnery, 1998.

Burtchaell, James T. *The Dying of the Light: The Disengagement of Colleges and Universities from their Churches*. Grand Rapids: Eerdmans, 2001.

Carmody, Denise. *Organizing a Christian Mind: A Theology of Higher Education*. Valley Forge, PA: Trinity, 1996.

Carpenter, Joel, and Kenneth W. Shipps, eds. *Making Higher Education Christian*. Grand Rapids: Eerdmans, 1987.

Claerbaut, David. *Faith and Learning on the Edge: A Bold Look at Religion in Higher Education*. Grand Rapids: Zondervan, 2004.

Clark, Burton. *The Distinctive College*. Chicago: Aldine, 1970.

Dockery, David S., and David P. Gushee, eds. *The Future of Christian Higher Education*. Nashville: Broadman & Holman, 1999.

Gill, David W., ed. *The Opening of the Christian Mind*. Downers Grove: InterVarsity, 1989.

_____. *Should God Get Tenure?* Grand Rapids: Eerdmans, 1997.

Glaspey, Terry W. *Great Books of the Christian Tradition*. Eugene, OR: Harvest House, 1996.

Gleason, Philip. *Contending with Modernity: Catholic Higher Education in the 20th Century*. New York: Oxford University Press, 1995.

Graff, Gerald. *Clueless in Academe: How Schooling Obscures the Life of the Mind*. New Haven: Yale University Press, 2003.

Haynes, Stephen R. *Professing in the Postmodern Academy: Faculty and the Future of Church-Related Colleges*. Waco: Baylor University Press, 2002.

Heie, Harold, and David Wolfe, eds. *The Reality of Christian Learning: Strategies for Faith-Learning Integration*. Grand Rapids: Eerdmans, 1987.

Henry, Doug, and Bob Agee, eds. *Faithful Learning and the Christian Scholarly Vocation*. Grand Rapids: Eerdmans, 2003.

Holmes, Arthur. *The Idea of a Christian College*. Grand Rapids: Eerdmans, 1975.

Hughes, Richard T., and William Adrian, eds. *Models for Christian Higher Education*. Grand Rapids: Eerdmans, 1997.

Jacobsen, Douglas, and Rhonda Hustdet, eds. *Scholarship and Christian Faith*. Oxford: Oxford University Press, 2004.

Lewis, Harry R. *Excellence without a Soul: How a Great University Forgot Education*. New York: Public Affairs, 2006.

Lickona, Thomas. *Educating for Character*. New York: Bantam, 1991.

Lockerbie, D. Bruce. *A Passion for Learning: The History of Christian Thought on Education*. Chicago: Moody, 1994.

Malik, Charles Habib. *A Christian Critique of the University*. Downers Grove: InterVarsity, 1982.

Mannoia, James. *Christian Liberal Arts: An Education That Goes Beyond*. Rowman & Littlefield, 2000.

Marsden, George. *The Outrageous Idea of Christian Scholarship*. New York: Oxford University Press, 1997.

_____. *The Soul of the American University*. New York: Oxford University Press, 1994.

_____, and Bradley J. Longfield, eds. *The Secularization of the Academy*. New York: Oxford University Press, 1992.

Moore, Steve, ed. *The University through the Eyes of Faith*. Indianapolis: Light & Life, 1998.

Newman, John Henry. *The Idea of a University*. Notre Dame: University of Notre Dame Press, reprint 1982.

Noll, Mark. *The Scandal of the Evangelical Mind*. Grand Rapids: Eerdmans, 1994.

Palmer, Parker. *To Know as We Are Known: A Spirituality of Education*. San Francisco: Harper & Row, 1983.

Pelikan, Jaroslav. *The Idea of the University: A Re-examination*. New Haven: Yale University Press, 1992.

Petersen, Michael. *With All Your Mind: A Christian Philosophy of Education*. Notre Dame, IN: University of Notre Dame Press, 2001.

Plantinga, Alvin. *The Twin Pillars of Christian Scholarship*. Grand Rapids: Calvin College, 1991.

Plantinga, Cornelius. *Engaging God's World: A Christian Vision of Faith, Learning and Living*. Grand Rapids: Eerdmans, 2002.

Poe, Harry L. *Christianity in the Academy*. Grand Rapids: Baker, 2004.

Power, R. Clark, and Daniel Lapsley, eds. *The Challenge of Pluralism: Education, Politics, and Values*. Notre Dame: University of Notre Dame Press, 1992.

Ringenberg, William C. *The Christian College: A History of Protestant Higher Education in America*. Grand Rapids: Baker, 2006.

Schmeltekopf, Donald D., and Dianna Vitunza, eds. *The Future of Baptist Higher Education*. Waco: Baylor University Press, 2006.

Schwehn, Mark R. *Exiles from Eden: Religion and the Academic Vocation in America*. New York: Oxford University Press, 1993.

Sommerville, John. *The Decline of the Secular University: Why the Academy Needs Religion*. Oxford: Oxford University Press, 2006.

Sterk, Andrea, and Nicholas Wolterstorff. *Religion, Scholarship, and Higher Education*. Notre Dame: University of Notre Dame Press, 2002.

Stevenson, Louise L. *Scholarly Means to Evangelical Ends: New Haven Scholars and the Transformation of Higher Education in America, 1830–1890*. Baltimore: Johns Hopkins University Press, 1986.

Trueblood, Elton. *The Idea of a College*. New York: Harper & Row, 1959.

Wells, Ronald, ed. *Keeping the Faith: Embracing the Tensions in Higher Education*. Grand Rapids: Eerdmans, 1996.

Williams, Clifford. *The Life of the Mind.* Grand Rapids: Baker, 2002.

Willimon, William H., and Thomas H. Naylor. *The Abandoned Generation: Rethinking Higher Education.* Grand Rapids: Eerdmans, 1995.

Wilkes, Peter. *Christianity Challenges the University.* Downers Grove: InterVarsity, 1981.

Wilson, Doug. *Recovering the Lost Tools of Learning.* Wheaton: Crossway, 1991.

Wolterstorff, Nicholas. *Educating for Shalom: Essays on Christian Higher Education.* Grand Rapids: Eerdmans, 2004.

Law and Political Science

Budziszewski, J. *Written on the Heart: The Case for Natural Law.* Downers Grove: InterVarsity, 1997.

Buzzard, Lynn Robert. *Christian Perspectives on Law and Justice.* Springfield, VA: Christian Legal Society, 1976.

Carter, Stephen L. *The Culture of Disbelief: How American Law and Politics Trivialize Religious Devotion.* San Francisco: Basic Books, 1993.

_____. *Integrity.* New York: Harper Collins, 1996.

Charles, Daryl. *Between Pacificism and Jihad: Just War and the Christian Tradition.* Downers Grove: InterVarsity, 2005.

Clements, Keith. *Learning to Speak: The Church's Voice in Public Affairs.* Edinburgh: T&T Clark, 1995.

Dooyeweerd, Herman. *Essays in Legal, Social, and Political Philosophy.* Lewiston, NY: Edwin Mellen Press, 2001.

Eidsmoe, John. *Christianity and the Constitution.* Grand Rapids: Baker, 1987.

Ellul, Jacques. *The Politics of God and the Politics of Man.* Grand Rapids: Eerdmans, 1972.

Elshtain, Jean Bethke. *Augustine and the Limits of Politics*. Notre Dame: University of Notre Dame Press, 1996.

_____. *Real Politics: Political Theory and Everyday Life*. Baltimore: Johns Hopkins University Press, 1997.

Finnis, John. *Natural Law and Natural Rights*. Oxford: Clarendon, 1980.

Gaede, S. D. *When Tolerance Is No Virtue*. Downers Grove: InterVarsity, 1993.

George, Robert P. *The Clash of Orthodoxies: Law, Religion, and Morality in Crisis*. Wilmington: ISI, 2001.

_____. *Making Men Moral: Civil Liberties and Public Morality*. Oxford: Oxford University Press, 1995.

_____, and Christopher Wolfe, eds. *Natural Law and Public Reason*. Washington, DC: Georgetown University Press, 2000.

Gushee, David, ed. *Christians and Politics: Beyond the Culture Wars*. Grand Rapids: Baker, 2000.

_____, ed. *Toward a Just and Caring Society*. Grand Rapids: Baker, 1999.

Hatch, Nathan. *The Democratization of American Christianity*. New Haven: Yale University Press, 1991.

Henry, Carl F. H. *Has Democracy Had Its Day?* Nashville: ERLC, 1996.

Howard, Philip K. *The Death of Common Sense: How Law Is Suffocating America*. New York: Random House, 1994.

Maclear, J. F., ed. *Church and State in the Modern Age*. Oxford: Oxford University Press, 1995.

Marshall, Paul. *Thine Is the Kingdom: A Biblical Perspective on Government and Politics Today*. Grand Rapids: Eerdmans, 1984.

Monsma, Stephen V. *Positive Neutrality*. Grand Rapids: Baker, 1993.

_____, *Pursuing Justice in a Sinful World*. Grand Rapids: Eerdmans, 1984.

Mouw, Richard. *Politics and the Biblical Drama*. Grand Rapids: Baker, 1983.

Neuhaus, Richard J. *The Naked Public Square: Religion and Democracy in America*. Grand Rapids: Eerdmans, 1984.

O'Donovan, Joan Lockwood. *Theology of Law and Authority in the English Reformation*. Atlanta: Emory University Press, 1991.

O'Donovan, Oliver. *The Desire of the Nations: Rediscovering the Roots of Political Theory*. Cambridge: Cambridge University Press, 1999.

_____, and Joan Lockwood O'Donovan. *Bonds of Imperfection: Christian Politics, Past and Present*. Grand Rapids: Eerdmans, 2004.

_____. *From Irenaeus to Grotius: A Sourcebook in Christian Political Thought*. Grand Rapids: Eerdmans, 1999.

Schlossberg, Herbert. *Idols for Destruction: Christian Faith and Its Confrontation with American Society*. Nashville: Thomas Nelson, 1983.

Sider, Ronald J., and Diane Knippers. *Toward an Evangelical Public Policy*. Grand Rapids: Baker, 2005.

Simon, Arthur. *Christian Faith and Public Policy*. Grand Rapids: Eerdmans, 1987.

Skillen, James. *Recharging the American Experiment*. Grand Rapids: Baker, 1994.

Smidt, Corwin E., ed. *Pulpit and Politics*. Waco: Baylor University Press, 2004.

Wolterstorff, Nicholas. *Until Justice and Peace Embrace*. Grand Rapids: Eerdmans, 1984.

Yoder, John Howard. *The Politics of Jesus*. Grand Rapids: Eerdmans, 1994.

Mathematics, Computer Science, and Engineering

Baker, T., and C. Jongsma. *The Shape and Number of Things.* Toronto: Development Center, 1981.

Barker, Stephen F. *Philosophy of Mathematics.* Englewood Cliffs, NJ: Prentice-Hall, 1964.

Borgman, Albert. *Crossing the Postmodern Divide.* Chicago: University of Chicago Press, 1992.

Brabenac, R. L. *A Christian Perspective on the Foundations of Mathematics.* Wheaton: Wheaton College, 1977.

Davis, Philip J., and Reuben Hersh. *The Mathematical Experience.* Boston: Birkhäuser Boston, 1981.

Edgar, Stacy. *Morality and Machines: Perspectives on Computer Ethics.* Boston: Jones & Bartlett, 1996.

Ellul, Jacques. *The Technological Society.* New York: Random, 1967.

Emerson, Allen, and Cheryl Forbes. *The Invasion of the Computer Culture.* Downers Grove: InterVarsity, 1989.

Ermann, M., Mary Williams, and Nichelle Shaul. *Computers, Ethics and Society.* New York: Oxford University Press, 1997.

Granville, H., Jr. *Logos: Mathematics and Christian Theology.* Lewisburg, PA: Bucknell University Press, 1976.

Groothius, Douglas. *The Soul in Cyberspace.* Grand Rapids: Baker, 1997.

Howell, Russell, and James Bradley, eds. *Mathematics in a Postmodern Age: A Christian Perspective.* Grand Rapids: Eerdmans, 2001.

Huntley, H. E. *The Divine Proportion: A Study in Mathematical Beauty.* New York: Dover, 1970.

Kline, Morris. *Mathematical Thought from Ancient to Modern Times.* Oxford: Oxford University Press, 1972.

Lyon, David. *The Information Society*. New York: Basil Blackwell, 1988.

_____. *The Silicon Society*. Grand Rapids: Eerdmans, 1986.

Mitcham, Carl, and Tim Grote. *Theology and Technology: Essays in Christian Analysis and Engineering*. Lanham, MD: University Press of America, 1984.

Monsma, Stephen V., ed. *Responsible Technology*. Grand Rapids: Eerdmans, 1986.

Postman, Neil. *Technopoly: The Surrender of Culture to Technology*. New York: Vintage, 1993.

Education

Brueggemann, Walter. *The Creative Word: Canon as a Model for Biblical Education*. Philadelphia: Fortress, 1982.

Burgess, W. Harold. *Models of Religious Education*. Wheaton: Victor, 1996.

Gangel, Kenneth O., and Warren S. Benson. *Christian Education: Its History and Philosophy*. Chicago: Moody, 1983.

Groome, Thomas. *Christian Religious Education*. New York: Harper & Row, 1980.

Habermas, Ronald, and Klaus Issler. *Teaching for Reconciliation*. Grand Rapids: Baker, 1992.

Healy, Jane M. *Endangered Minds: Why Children Don't Think and What We Can Do about It*. New York: Simon & Schuster, 1990.

Hill, Brian V. *Faith at the Blackboard: Issues Facing the Christian Teacher*. Grand Rapids: Eerdmans, 1982.

Hirsch, E. D., Jr. *The Schools We Need and Why We Don't Have Them*. New York: Doubleday, 1996.

Issler, Klaus, and Ronald Habermas. *How We Learn*. Grand Rapids: Baker, 1994.

Kilpatrick, William. *Why Johnny Can't Tell Right from Wrong: What We Can Do about It.* New York: Simon & Schuster, 1992.

Miller, Donald E. *Story and Context: An Introduction to Christian Education.* Nashville: Abingdon, 1987.

Pazmino, Robert. *Foundational Issues in Christian Education.* Grand Rapids: Baker, 1988.

Peterson, Michael. *Philosophy of Education.* Downers Grove: InterVarsity, 1986.

Purpel, David E. *The Moral and Spiritual Crisis in Education.* Granby, MA: Bergin & Garvey, 1989.

Roques, Mark. *Curriculum Unmasked: Towards a Christian Understanding of Education.* London: Monarch, 1989.

Runner, H. Evan. *The Relation of the Bible to Learning.* Jordan Station, ON: Paideia, 1982.

Sowell, Thomas. *Inside American Education: The Decline, the Deception, the Dogmas.* New York: Free Press, 1993.

Steensma, Geraldine, ed. *Shaping School Curriculum: A Biblical View.* Terre Haute, IN: Signal, 1977.

Veith, Gene E. *Classical Education: Towards the Revival of American Schooling.* Washington, DC: Capital Research Center, 1998.

Wolterstorff, Nicholas. *Educating for Responsible Action.* Grand Rapids: Eerdmans, 1982.

History

Bauman, Michael, and Martin I. Klauber, eds. *Historians of the Christian Tradition.* Nashville: Broadman & Holman, 1995.

Bebbington, David W. *Patterns in History.* Downers Grove: InterVarsity, 1980.

Butterfield, Herbert. *Christianity and History.* London: Bell, 1949.

_____. *Writings on Christianity and History*. Edited by C. T. McIntire. New York: Oxford University Press, 1979.

Kuklick, Bruce, and D. G. Hart, eds. *Religious Advocacy and American History*. Grand Rapids: Eerdmans, 1997.

Marsden, George, and Frank Roberts, eds. *A Christian View of History*. Grand Rapids: Eerdmans, 1975.

McIntire, C. T., ed. *God, History and Historians: Modern Christian Views of History*. New York: Oxford University Press, 1977.

_____, and Ronald Wells, eds. *History and Historical Understanding*. Grand Rapids: Eerdmans, 1984.

Noll, Mark. *Turning Points: Decisive Moments in the History of Christianity*. Downers Grove: InterVarsity, 1997.

Swanstrom, R. *History in the Making*. Downers Grove: InterVarsity, 1978.

Wells, Ronald, ed. *History and Historical Understanding*. Grand Rapids: Eerdmans, 1984.

_____. *History through the Eyes of Faith*. San Francisco: Harper & Row, 1989.

Language, Linguistics, and International Studies

Grunlan, Stephen, and Marvin Mayers. *Cultural Anthropology: A Christian Perspective*. Grand Rapids: Zondervan, 1988.

Heibert, Paul. *Anthropological Insights for Missionaries*. Grand Rapids: Baker, 1985.

Kraft, C. *Anthropology for Christian Witness*. Maryknoll, NY: Orbis, 1997.

Larkin, William J. *Culture and Biblical Hermeneutics*. Grand Rapids: Baker, 1988.

Lingenfelter, Sherwood. *Agents of Transformation*. Grand Rapids: Baker, 1996.

_____. *Transforming Culture*. Grand Rapids: Baker, 1992.

Longacre, Robert E. *Grammar of Discourse*. New York: Plenum, 1996.

Nida, Eugene. *Religion across Culture*. New York: Harper, 1968.

Pike, Kenneth L. *Linguistic Concepts*. Lincoln: University of Nebraska Press, 1982.

_____, and Evelyn G. Pike. *Grammatical Analysis*. Dallas: Summer Institute of Linguistics and University of Texas at Arlington, 1977.

Sanneh, Lamin. *Translating the Message*. Maryknoll, NY: Orbis, 1989.

Silva, Moises. *God, Language, and Scripture: Reading the Bible in the Light of General Linguistics*. Grand Rapids: Zondervan, 1990.

Literature

Barratt, David, Roger Pooley, and Leland Ryken, eds. *The Discerning Reader: Christian Perspectives on Literature and Theory*. Leicester: Apollos, 1995.

Buechner, Frederick. *The Clown in the Bellfry: Writings on Faith and Fiction*. San Francisco: Harper, 1992.

Dillard, Annie. *Living by Fiction*. San Francisco: Harper & Row, 1982.

Edwards, Bruce L. *A Rhetoric of Reading: C. S. Lewis' Defense of Western Literacy*. Provo, UT: BYU Press, 1986.

_____. *The Taste of the Pineapple: Essays on C. S. Lewis as Critic, Reader and Imagination Writer*. Bowling Green, KY: Popular Press, 1988.

_____, Thomas Klein, and Thomas Wymer. *Searching for Great Ideas: Conversations between Past and Present*. New York: Harcourt, 1997.

Eliot, T. S. *Christianity and Culture*. New York: Harcourt Brace, 1940.

Ericson, E. E., Jr., and G. B. Tennyson, eds. *Religion and Modern Literature: Essays in Theory and Criticism*. Grand Rapids: Eerdmans, 1975.

Hirsch, E. D. *Aims of Interpretation*. Chicago: University of Chicago Press, 1976.

_____. *Validity in Interpretation*. New Haven: Yale University Press, 1967.

Jeffrey, David L. *People of the Book: Christian Identity and Literary Culture*. Grand Rapids: Eerdmans, 1996.

Lewis, C. S. *Studies in Words*. Cambridge: Cambridge University Press, 1974.

Lundin, Roger, and Susan Gallagher. *Literature through the Eyes of Faith*. San Francisco: Harper & Row, 1989.

Norris, Christopher. *The Truth about Postmodernism*. Oxford: Blackwell, 1993.

Ricouer, Paul. *Figuring the Sacred*. Minneapolis: Fortress, 1995.

Ryken, Leland, ed. *The Christian Imagination: Essays on Literature and the Arts*. Grand Rapids: Baker, 1981.

_____. *Triumphs of the Imagination*. Downers Grove: InterVarsity, 1979.

Sayers, Dorothy. *The Mind of the Maker*. London: Methuen, 1947.

TeSelle, S. F. *Literature and the Christian Life*. New Haven: Yale University Press, 1966.

Timmerman, John, and Donald Hettinga. *In the World: Reading and Writing as a Christian*. Grand Rapids: Baker, 1987.

Walhout, Clarence, and Leland Ryken, eds. *Contemporary Literary Theory: A Christian Appraisal*. Grand Rapids: Eerdmans 1991.

Willimon, William H. *Reading with Deeper Eyes*. Nashville: Upper Room, 1998.

Philosophy/Ethics

Abraham, William. *An Introduction to the Philosophy of Religion*. New York: Prentice-Hall, 1985.

Audi, Robert, ed. *The Cambridge Dictionary of Philosophy*. Cambridge: Cambridge University Press, 1995.

Beckwith, Francis J. *Do the Right Thing*. Boston: Jones & Bartlett, 1996.

Brown, Colin. *Christianity and Western Thought*. Downers Grove: InterVarsity, 1990.

_____. *Philosophy and the Christian Faith*. Downers Grove: InterVarsity, 1968.

Chamberlain, Paul. *Can We Be Good without God?* Downers Grove: InterVarsity, 1996.

Clark, David, and Robert Rakestraw. *Readings in Christian Ethics*. 2 vols. Grand Rapids: Baker, 1994.

Clark, Kelly James, ed. *Philosophers Who Believe*. Downers Grove: InterVarsity, 1993.

Dooyeweerd, Herman. *In the Twilight of Western Thought*. Nutley: Craig, 1968.

Evans, C. Stephen. *Philosophy of Religion*. Downers Grove: InterVarsity, 1982.

Feinberg, John, and Paul Feinberg. *Ethics for a Brave New World*. Wheaton: Crossway, 1996.

Gagnon, Robert. *The Bible and Homosexual Practice*. Nashville: Abingdon, 2002.

Geisler, Norman L. *Christian Ethics: Options and Issues*. Grand Rapids: Baker, 1989.

Geivett, R. Douglas, and Brendan Sweetman, eds. *Contemporary Perspectives on Religious Epistemology*. New York: Oxford University Press, 1992.

Grenz, Stanley. *The Moral Quest*. Downers Grove: InterVarsity, 1998.

Gushee, David P. *The Righteous Gentiles of the Holocaust*. Philadelphia: Fortress, 1993.

Hays, Richard. *The Moral Vision of the New Testament*. San Francisco: Harper, 1996.

Henry, Carl F. H. *Christian Personal Ethics*. Grand Rapids: Eerdmans, 1957.

Holmes, Arthur. *Philosophy: A Christian Perspective*. Downers Grove: InterVarsity, 1975.

Kreeft, Peter. *Between Heaven and Hell*. Downers Grove: InterVarsity, 1988.

Lewis, C. S. *The Pilgrim's Regress*. Grand Rapids: Eerdmans, 1979. First published 1933.

_____. *The Problem of Pain*. New York: Macmillan, 1994. First published 1940.

Longenecker, Richard. *New Testament Social Ethics*. Grand Rapids: Eerdmans, 1984.

MacIntyre, Alasdair. *After Virtue: A Study in Moral Theory*. Notre Dame: University of Notre Dame Press, 1984.

Meilaender, Gilbert. *Faith and Faithfulness: Basic Themes in Christian Ethics*. Notre Dame: University of Notre Dame Press, 1991.

_____. *The Theory and Practice of Virtue*. Notre Dame: University of Notre Dame Press, 1981.

Morris, Thomas V., ed. *God and the Philosophers*. Oxford: Oxford University Press, 1994.

_____. *Making Sense of It All*. Grand Rapids: Eerdmans, 1992.

Plantinga, Alvin. *The Nature of Necessity*. Oxford: Clarendon, 1974.

Pojman, Louis P. *Ethics: Discovering Right and Wrong.* Belmont, CA: Wadsworth, 1995.

Rae, Scott. *Moral Choices.* Grand Rapids: Zondervan, 1995.

Sider, Ronald J. *Completely Pro-Life.* Downers Grove: InterVarsity, 1987.

Stassen, Glen, and David P. Gushee. *Kingdom Ethics.* Downers Grove: InterVarsity, 2003.

Stott, John R. W. *Involvement.* Old Tappan, NJ: Revell, 1984.

Verhey, Allen. *The Great Reversal: Ethics and the New Testament.* Grand Rapids: Eerdmans, 1984.

Wolfe, David L. *Epistemology: The Justification of Belief.* Downers Grove: InterVarsity, 1982.

Wolters, Albert. *Our Place in the Philosophical Tradition.* Toronto: Institute for Christian Studies, 1975.

Wright, Christopher. *An Eye for an Eye: The Place of Old Testament Ethics Today.* Downers Grove: InterVarsity, 1983.

Yandell, Keith E. *Christianity and Philosophy.* Grand Rapids: Eerdmans, 1984.

Psychology

Benner, David, ed. *Baker Encyclopedia of Psychology.* Grand Rapids: Baker, 1985.

Blazer, Don. *Freud vs. God: How Psychiatry Lost Its Soul and Christianity Lost Its Mind.* Downers Grove: InterVarsity, 1998.

Boyd, Jeffrey. *Reclaiming the Soul: The Search for Meaning in a Self-Centered Culture.* Cleveland: Pilgrim, 1996.

Carter, John D., and Bruce Narramore. *Integration of Psychology and Theology.* Grand Rapids: Zondervan, 1979.

Dueck, Alvin. *Between Jerusalem and Athens: Ethical Perspectives on Culture, Religion, and Psychotherapy.* Grand Rapids: Baker, 1995.

Evans, C. Stephen. *Wisdom and Humanness in Psychology: Prospects for a Christian Approach*. Grand Rapids: Baker, 1989.

Farnsworth, Kirk. *Wholehearted Integration: Harmonizing Psychology and Christianity through Word and Deed*. Grand Rapids: Baker, 1985.

Jeeves, Malcom A., and David Myers. *Psychology through the Eyes of Faith*. San Francisco: Harper & Row, 1989.

Jones, Stanton L., ed. *Psychology and the Christian Faith*. Grand Rapids: Baker, 1986.

Moreland, J. P., and David M. Ciocchi, eds. *Christian Perspectives on Being Human*. Grand Rapids: Baker, 1993.

Swinburne, Richard. *The Evolution of the Soul*. Oxford: Clarendon, 1986.

Van Leeuwen, Mary Stewart. *The Sorcerer's Apprentice: A Christian Looks at the Changing Face of Psychology*. Downers Grove: InterVarsity, 1983.

Vitz, Paul. *Psychology as Religion: The Cult of Self-Worship*. Grand Rapids: Eerdmans, 1994.

Health Care and Biomedical Ethics

Allen, David E., L. P. Bird, and Robert Hermann, eds. *Whole Person Medicine*. Downers Grove: InterVarsity, 1980.

Ashley, Benedict M., and Kevin D. O'Rourke. *Health Care Ethics: A Theological Analysis*. St. Louis: Catholic Health Association of the United States, 1982.

Beckwith, Francis J. *Politically Correct Death*. Grand Rapids: Baker, 1992.

Bouma, Hessel, and et al. *Christian Faith, Health, and Medical Practice*. Grand Rapids: Eerdmans, 1989.

Carson, Verna B. *Spiritual Dimensions of Nursing Practice*. Philadelphia: W. B. Saunders, 1989.

Fournier, Keith A., and William D. Watkins. *In Defense of Life.* Colorado Springs: NavPress, 1996.

Granberg-Michaelson, Karin. *In the Land of the Living: Health Care and the Church.* Grand Rapids: Zondervan, 1984.

Kilner, John F. *Life on the Line.* Grand Rapids: Eerdmans, 1992.

_____, Nigel M. DeS. Cameron, and David Schiedermayer, eds. *A Philosophical Basis of Medical Practice.* New York: Oxford University Press, 1981.

Lammers, Stephen E., and Allen Verhey. *On Moral Medicine: Theological Perspectives in Medical Ethics.* Grand Rapids: Eerdmans, 1987.

Larson, Edward J., and Darrel W. Amundsen. *A Different Death: Euthanasia & the Christian Tradition.* Downers Grove: InterVarsity, 1998.

Meilaender, Gilbert. *Bioethics: A Primer for Christians.* Grand Rapids: Eerdmans, 1996.

_____. *Body, Soul, and Bioethics.* Notre Dame: University of Notre Dame Press, 1996.

Moreland, J. P. *The Life and Death Debate.* Westport, CT: Praeger, 1990.

O'Brien, Mary Elizabeth. *Spirituality in Nursing.* Sudbury, MA: Jones & Bartlett, 1999.

Pellegrino, Edmund D., and David C. Thomasma. *For the Patient's Good.* New York: Oxford University Press, 1988.

_____. *A Philosophical Basis of Medical Practice.* New York: Oxford University Press, 1981.

Ram, Eric, ed. *Transforming Health: Christian Approaches to Healing and Wholeness.* Monrovia, CA: MARC, 1995.

Shelly, Judith Allen, and Arlene B. Miller. *Called to Care: A Christian Theology of Nursing.* Downers Grove: InterVarsity, 1999.

_____. *Values in Conflict: Christian Nursing in a Changing Profession*. Downers Grove: InterVarsity, 1991.

Science and Environmental Studies

Austin, Richard C. *Hope for the Land: Nature in the Bible*. Atlanta: John Knox, 1988.

Bailey, Lloyd R. *Genesis, Creation and Creationism*. Mahwah, NJ: Paulist, 1993.

Bakken, Peter W., Joan Gibb Engel, and J. Ronald Engel. *Ecology, Justice and Christian Faith: A Critical Guide to the Literature*. Westport, CT: Greenwood, 1995.

Barbour, Ian. *Issues in Science and Religion*. New York: Harper & Row, 1966.

Behe, Michael. *Darwin's Black Box*. New York: Free Press, 1996.

Brueggemann, Walter. *The Land: Place as Gift, Promise and Challenge in Biblical Faith*. Minneapolis: Fortress, 1977.

Coleman, William R. *Biology in the Nineteenth Century*. Cambridge: Cambridge University Press, 1977.

Corey, M. A. *God and the New Cosmology: The Anthropic Design Argument*. Boston: Rowman and Littlefield, 1993.

Craig, William Lane, and Quentin Smith. *Theism, Atheism, and Big Bang Cosmology*. Oxford: Clarendon, 1993.

Cromartie, Michael. *Creation at Risk? Religion, Science, and the Environment*. Grand Rapids: Eerdmans, 1995.

Dembski, William A., ed. *Darwin's Nemesis: Phillip Johnson and the Intelligent Design Movement*. Downers Grove: InterVarsity, 2006.

Denton, Michael. *Evolution: A Theory in Crisis*. London: Burnett, 1995.

DeWitt, Calvin B. *Earth-Wise: A Biblical Response to Environmental Issues*. Grand Rapids: CRC Publications, 1994.

_____. *The Environment and the Christian*. Grand Rapids: Baker, 1991.

_____, and Ghillean Prance, eds. *Missionary Earthkeeping*. Macon, GA: Mercer University Press, 1992.

Goodwin, B. C. *How the Leopard Changed Its Spots*. New York: Simon & Schuster, 1994.

Granberg-Michaelson, Wesley. *Ecology and Life: Accepting Our Environmental Responsibility*. Waco: Word, 1988.

Hall, Douglas John. *Imaging God: Dominion as Stewardship*. Grand Rapids: Eerdmans, 1986.

Harman, P. M. *Energy, Force, and Matter: A Historical Survey*. Cambridge: Cambridge University Press, 1982.

Hooykaas, R. *Religion and the Rise of Modern Science*. Grand Rapids: Eerdmans, 1972.

Hummel, Charles. *The Galileo Connection: Resolving Conflicts between Science and the Bible*. Downers Grove: InterVarsity, 1986.

Jaki, Stanley. *The Road of Science and the Ways of God*. Chicago: University of Chicago Press, 1980.

Johnson, Phillip. *Darwin on Trial*. Downers Grove: InterVarsity, 1991.

Kilner, J. F., Nigel M. De S. Cameron, D. L. Schiedermayer, eds. *Bioethics and the Future of Medicine: A Christian Appraisal*. Grand Rapids: Eerdmans, 1995.

Kirk, Janice E., and Donald R. Kirk. *Cherish the Earth: The Environment and Scripture*. Scottdale, PA: Herald, 1993.

Kuhn, Thomas. *The Structure of Scientific Revolutions*. Chicago: University of Chicago Press, 1970. First published 1962.

Land, Richard D., and Louis Moore, eds. *The Earth Is the Lord's*. Nashville: Broadman & Holman, 1991.

LeQuire, Stan L., ed. *The Best Preaching on Earth: Sermons on Caring for Creation*. Valley Forge, PA: Judson, 1996.

Lindberg, David C., and Ronald C. Numbers, eds. *God and Nature*. Berkeley: University of California Press, 1986.

MacKay, Donald. *The Clockwork Image*. Downers Grove: InterVarsity, 1974.

Marsch, Glenn. *Enlightened Hearts and Cynical Eyes: Why Christian Faith and Doctrine Are Critical Scientific Tools*. Washington, DC: CCCU, 1997. http://www1.gospelcom.net/cccu/re-search/projects/marshprj.html.

McGrath, Alister. *Dawkins' God*. Oxford: Blackwell, 2004.

Meyer, Art, and Jocele Meyer. *Earthkeepers: Environmental Perspectives on Hunger, Poverty and Injustice*. Scottdale, PA: Herald, 1991.

Moreland, J. P. *Christianity and the Nature of Science*. Grand Rapids: Baker, 1989.

_____, ed. *The Creation Hypothesis*. Downers Grove: InterVarsity, 1993.

Morris, Henry. *Scientific Creationism*. El Cajon, CA: Master, 1985.

Pearcey, Nancy R., and Charles Thaxton. *The Soul of Science*. Wheaton: Crossway, 1994.

Poe, Harry, and Jimmy H. Davis. *Designer Universe*. Nashville: Broadman & Holman, 2002.

_____. *Science and Faith: An Evangelical Dialogue*. Nashville: Broadman & Holman, 2000.

Polanyi, Michael. *The Tacit Dimension*. Garden City, NY: Doubleday, 1967.

Polkinghorne, John. *The Faith of a Physicist*. Minneapolis: Fortress, 1994.

Pollard, W. *Physicist and Christian*. Greenwich, CT: Seabury, 1961.

Ratzsch, Del. *The Battle of Beginnings: Why Neither Side Is Winning the Creation Evolution Debate*. Downers Grove: InterVarsity, 1996.

_____. *Philosophy of Science.* Downers Grove: InterVarsity, 1986.

Reichenbach, Bruce R., and E. V. Anderson. *On Behalf of God: A Christian Ethic for Biology.* Grand Rapids: Eerdmans, 1995.

Ross, Hugh. *The Creator and the Cosmos.* Colorado Springs, CO: NavPress, 1993.

_____. *The Fingerprint of God.* Orange, CA: Promise, 1989.

Russell, R. J., et al. *Physics, Philosophy, and Theology: A Common Quest for Understanding.* Notre Dame: University of Notre Dame Press, 1988.

Schaeffer, Francis. *Pollution and the Death of Man.* Wheaton: Tyndale, 1970.

Sheldon, Joseph K. *Rediscovery of Creation: A Bibliographic Study of the Church's Response to the Environmental Crisis.* ATLA Bibliography Series 29. Metuchen, NJ: Scarecrow, 1992.

Templeton, John, and Robert Herman. *The God Who Would Be Known: Divine Revelations in Contemporary Science.* San Francisco: Harper, 1988.

Thaxton, Charles, and Walter Bradley. *The Mystery of Life's Origin: Reassessing Current Theories.* Wheaton: Crossway, 1984.

Val Til, Howard. *The Fourth Day: What the Bible and Heavens Are Telling Us about Creation.* Grand Rapids: Eerdmans, 1986.

_____, Davis A. Young, and Clarence Merringa. *Science Held Hostage.* Downers Grove: InterVarsity, 1988.

Van Dyke, Fred, David C. Mahan, Joseph K. Sheldon, and Raymond Brand. *Redeeming Creation: The Biblical Basis for Environmental Stewardship.* Downers Grove: InterVarsity, 1996.

Wilkinson, Loren, ed. *Earthkeeping in the Nineties: Stewardship of Creation.* Grand Rapids: Eerdmans, 1991.

Wright, Richard T. *Biology Through the Eyes of Faith*. San Francisco: Harper & Row, 1989.

Young, Richard A. *Healing the Earth*. Nashville: Broadman & Holman, 1994.

Social Science/Social Work

Barrett, William. *Death of the Soul: From Descartes to the Computer*. New York: Anchor, 1986.

Bellah, Robert, et al. *Habits of the Heart: Individualism and Commitment in American Life*. Berkeley: University of California Press, 1985.

Berger, Peter. *The Desecularization of the World: Resurgent Religion and World Politics*. Grand Rapids: Eerdmans, 1999.

_____. *Facing Up to Modernity: Excursions in Society, Religion, and Politics*. New York: Basic, 1977.

_____. *The Sacred Canopy: Elements of a Sociological Theory of Religion*. Garden City, NY: Doubleday, 1967.

Campolo, Tony. *Growing Up in America*. Grand Rapids: Zondervan, 1989.

_____, and David A. Fraser. *Sociology through the Eyes of Faith*. San Francisco: Harper & Row, 1992.

DeSanto C., Z. Lindblade, and M. Poloma, eds. *Christian Perspectives on Social Problems*. Indianapolis: Wesley, 1992.

Ellul, Jacques. *The Subversion of Christianity*. Grand Rapids: Eerdmans, 1986.

_____. *The Technological Society*. Grand Rapids: Eerdmans, 1990.

Grunlar, Stephen, and M. Reimer, eds. *Christian Perspectives on Sociology*. Grand Rapids: Zondervan, 1982.

Hugen, Beryl, ed. *Christianity and Social Work: Readings on the Integration of Christian Faith and Social Work Practice*.

Butsford, CT: North American Association of Christians in Social Work, 1998.

Hunter, James Davidson. *Culture Wars*. New York: Harper Collins, 1991.

_____. *Evangelicalism*. Chicago: University of Chicago Press, 1987.

Lyon, David. *Christians and Sociology*. Downers Grove: InterVarsity, 1975.

Perkins, John M. *Beyond Charity: The Call to Christian Community Development*. Grand Rapids: Baker, 1993.

Perkins, Richard. *Looking Both Ways: Exploring the Interface between Christianity and Sociology*. Grand Rapids: Baker, 1987.

Perkins, Spencer, and Chris Rice. *More than Equals: Racial Healing for the Sake of the Gospel*. Downers Grove: InterVarsity, 1993.

Storkey, Alan. *A Christian Social Perspective*. Leicester, England: InterVarsity, 1979.

Weber, Max. *The Sociology of Religion*. Translated by E. Fischoff. Boston: Beacon, 1993.

Woodley, Randy. *Living in Color: Embracing God's Passion for Ethnic Diversity*. Downers Grove: InterVarsity, 2001.

Wuthnow, Robert. *America and the Challenges of Religious Diversity*. Princeton: Princeton University Press, 2005.

_____. *God and Mammon in America*. New York: Free Press, 1994.

_____. *The Restructuring of American Religion*. Princeton: Princeton University Press, 1990.

_____, ed. *Rethinking Materialism*. Grand Rapids: Eerdmans, 1995.

Yancey, George. *Beyond Racial Gridlock: Embracing Mutual Responsibility*. Downers Grove: InterVarsity, 2006.

Athletics, Physical Education, and Wellness

Baum, Gregory, and John Coleman, eds. *Sport*. Edinburgh: T&T Clark, 1989.

Blaylock, Mike. *The Right Way to Win*. Chicago: Moody, 1990.

Covey, Richard. *Happiness Is Being a Physically Fit Christian*. Nashville: Broadman & Holman, 1989.

_____. *Nutrition for God's Temple*. Nashville: LifeWay, 1994.

Higgs, Robert J. *God in the Stadium: Sports and Religion in America*. Lexington: University of Kentucky Press, 1995.

Hoffman, Shirl J., ed. *Sport and Religion*. Champaign, IL: Human Kinetics, 1992.

Hubbard, Steve. *Faith in Sports: Athletes and Their Religion On and Off the Court*. New York: Doubleday, 1998.

Prebish, Charles S. *Religion and Sport: The Meeting of Sacred and Profane*. Westport, CT: Greenwood, 1993.

Richardson, Bobby. *Grand Slam: Principles of Baseball and the Christian Life*. Atlanta: Crossroads, 1978.

Warner, Gary. *Competition: What Is It Doing to Us?* Elgin, IL: Cook, 1979.

Wilhelmi, Norm. *The Sweet Smell of Pine*. Mt. Juliet, TN: Cross Reference, 1993.

Name Index

Subject Index

Scripture Index